Change Your

Thoughts,

Change Your

Life

Change Your Thoughts, Change Your Life

DR. DAVID STOOP

© 2014 by Dr. David Stoop

Published by Revell
a division of Baker Publishing Group
PO Box 6287, Grand Rapids, MI 49516-6287
www.revellbooks.com

Spire edition published 2018

ISBN 978-0-8007-2966-0

Previously printed under the title *Rethink How You Think*

Printed in the United States of America

Unless otherwise indicated, Scripture quotations are from the *Holy Bible*, New Living Translation, copyright © 1996, 2004, 2007 by Tyndale House Foundation. Used by permission of Tyndale House Publishers, Inc., Carol Stream, Illinois 60188. All rights reserved.

Scripture quotations marked KJV are from the King James Version of the Bible.

Scripture quotations marked NIV are from the Holy Bible, New International Version®. NIV®. Copyright © 1973, 1978, 1984, 2011 by Biblica, Inc.™ Used by permission of Zondervan. All rights reserved worldwide. www.zondervan.com

The author is represented by and this book is published in association with the literary agency of WordServe Literary Group, Ltd., www.wordserveliterary.com.

To protect the privacy of those who have shared their stories with the author, some details and names have been changed.

All italics used in Scripture are the author's emphasis.

20 21 22 23 24   7 6 5 4

Those who are dominated by the sinful nature think about sinful things, but those who are controlled by the Holy Spirit think about things that please the Spirit. So letting your sinful nature control your minds leads to death. But letting the Spirit control your mind leads to life and peace.

~ Romans 8:5–6

Contents

Part 1

The unifying word for our world today is *stress*. It is a common condition that affects us all, regardless of age. We want to be in control and we don't want to worry, but it seems that peace eludes us and stress overwhelms us. As Christians, we want the peace that Scripture describes as that which surpasses all understanding, but the harder we try to find it, the more we do not experience it. Why would the apostle Paul write so much about that kind of peace in the book of Philippians? What are we missing here? Why would he tell us we are to renew our minds in order to find that kind of peace? How does one go about such a process?

Paul gives us the outline in 2 Corinthians 10:3–5. He uses the metaphor of a battleground. We are to battle against the proud arguments that set themselves against God. Paul is echoing a theme found throughout the Bible—that there are two paths open to us. On one path, we believe those proud arguments against God, and on the other path, we think God's way. But how can we change paths?

The work being done by today's brain scientists can give us added insight into ways we can rethink how we think, and in doing so, we can unlock the power that God has made available to us when we hide his Word in our heart.

Part 1 describes some of the incredible things our brains can do—all of which are part of God's design. Like the psalmist David, you will be amazed at how wonderfully God has made each of us.

1

The Choice between Two Paths

The day I became a new father, I made a vow. Our first son had just been born, and I can remember it as if it were yesterday. After leaving the hospital, I parked the car and was walking to our apartment. Filled with joy, I exclaimed, "I've got a son! Wow!" My next thought was, *And I'm going to have a different relationship with him than my father had with me.* I made a serious vow that afternoon to change something about which I cared deeply.

As time passed, I remembered my vow. Over the years, I did all kinds of things with my firstborn, and later with his two brothers, that my father had never done with me. I remained determined to do things differently. Though my father took me to church, and faithfully at that, he never came to any school event. He never let me help him do work, like painting, around the house. He was always too busy, too impatient, or too tired. I understood his resources were limited because he worked long, hard hours in a factory. But understanding that didn't change the hurt and unfulfilled desire in my heart to have had a dad who was involved in my life. I felt as though he didn't accept me as a son.

It wasn't until my oldest son was graduating from high school that I realized I had failed miserably in fulfilling my vow. Though I had been involved in all kinds of ways in my sons' lives—going to all their school and sporting events, even coaching their Little League team—I really hadn't changed the *pattern* of my father's relationship with me: I had stayed emotionally disconnected from my sons. Though it appeared different on the outside, on an emotional level my relationship with them was no different than the empty relationship I had had with my own dad. My vow hadn't worked!

I was frustrated because I knew the verse in Scripture that says, "Anyone who belongs to Christ has become a new person. The old life is gone; a new life has begun!" (2 Cor. 5:17). Where was this new person I was supposed to be? I had placed my trust in Christ the summer after I graduated from high school. Then, soon after my first son was born, I entered the ministry, leading a parachurch youth program. Remembering my vow to be a different kind of father, I had prayed to be transformed.

As my sons were growing, I was busy doing "ministry" with other people's sons and daughters, unable to recognize the ways I'd imitated my father's pattern of non-involvement. Why wasn't I able to be different in the way I related with my sons? Why, even though I had made a very serious vow and worked hard at keeping it, did nothing change?

Have you ever had that kind of frustration in your life? Have you ever questioned why having a relationship with Christ really didn't change some important areas of your life?

Part of this struggle led me to write a book titled *You Are What You Think*. Over the years a lot of people have let me know that they have been helped by that little book. It says that if we can change the way we think, we can change the way we live. What's good news for some, though, sounds like bad news for others. Like me, many have discovered firsthand that changing the way you think and act is not always an easy task! We may *want* to change our thoughts and the resulting behaviors—especially those thoughts that lead to sinful behaviors—and we may even succeed for a short time. But then we seem to fall back into the old patterns again, frustrated at the lack of transformation in our lives. There has to be more. To get at the "more," we need to define just what it is that we need to change in order for our lives to be transformed.

Is Change Possible?

Have you ever vowed to change something in your life? Yet no matter how committed you were to making that change, nothing really changed, or the changes you did make didn't last very long. As a counselor, I'm often asked, "Can people really change?" Many today are frustrated when they're not able to bring about lasting changes in important areas of their own lives. Until recently, our inability to make changes was usually chalked up to weak willpower. Today, though, research is showing that the strength of our willpower is not the issue. Everyone's willpower eventually fails, and the old problems simply return. So then what is it that makes it so hard for us to achieve even the most desirable and critical changes in our lives?

The prophet Jeremiah gives us a vivid snapshot of how hard it is for people to change, even when they are facing disaster. He was called by God to warn the people of Israel of coming destruction. In spelling it out for his listeners as clearly as he could, Jeremiah delivered to them a universal principle. He said there were two paths—opposite paths!—open to all people, and that whether they knew it or not, they would choose one or the other. Jeremiah boldly announced, "Stand at the crossroads and look; ask for the ancient paths, ask where the good way is, and walk in it" (Jer. 6:16 NIV). Other translations call it the "godly way." In other words, Jeremiah is exhorting them—and us—to choose a path carefully!

Jeremiah continues to detail the benefits of walking on this ancient path. Promising peace, he offers of the good way, "Travel its path, and you will find rest for your souls." Rest for your souls! His words offer the relief for which we thirst. Two paths. We get to choose. In reality, we are choosing all the time which path to take. One path ends in destruction, and the culmination of the other ancient path is "rest for your souls." You might be scratching your head right now and wondering, "Why would these ancient travelers *not* choose the good way?" But just like us, the people of Jerusalem, out of selfish desires, made the wrong choice. Because they wouldn't change, they said to Jeremiah, "No, that's not the road we want!" (6:16).

And even though road signs all along the path they'd chosen warned "Death!" and "Destruction!"—while the road toward which Jeremiah pointed was marked "Rest" and "Peace"— they couldn't, or wouldn't, change paths.

It's the choice we've faced since the beginning of time. Our ancestors in the Garden of Eden chose the path of disobedience, and too often we blindly follow in their steps. We *read* in the Bible about the transformed life, but we fail to experience it. In frustration, most of us settle for a life filled with limits. Though we've tried to find peace in the midst of stress, time and time again it just hasn't worked. So we give up, and settling for what is, we accept what we call "reality."

But not everyone gives up. There are others, a lot like you and me, who still want and still believe that there is a different way to live life. The ancient biblical path hasn't been hidden away in some anachronistic dimension. It can be found and traveled today! Like me, you may have had your share of discouragement and frustration, but you still want to live out the reality of a transformed life. You may even believe it's possible because the Bible promises it, but like a traveler without a GPS, you just don't know how to get there. The words of Paul in Romans 12:2, that we are not to "copy the behavior and customs of this world, but let God transform [us] into a new person by changing the way [we] think," point us toward the godly way. The King James Version of Paul's exhortation instructs, "Do not be conformed to this world: but be ye transformed by the renewing of your mind." And while we long for transformation, yearning for changed lives, the truth is that we aren't even certain what a renewed mind looks like, or how it thinks.

Changed Hearts or Renewed Minds?

Let's look first at what really has to change. Paul tells us we are to renew our minds. That's clear enough, but Proverbs 23:7 mentions thoughts as being in our heart. The passage says, "For as he thinketh in his heart, so is he" (KJV). But don't minds *think* and hearts *feel*? How does a person think in his or her heart? To find out, one must understand what the Hebrew words translated as *heart* and *mind* meant to Paul, a Jew. The Hebrew word *lev*, used in Proverbs and elsewhere, is translated as "heart." But it is also translated as "mind" in other places! If you were a native Hebrew speaker, that wouldn't bother you. You'd think beyond either the singular word *heart* or *mind* to the actual meaning of the word. *Lev* could be translated more accurately as "the center of our being." So whenever you encounter either *heart* or *mind* in the Bible, if you think like a person who spoke Hebrew, you'd interpret the reference as "the center of our being." For example, you'd understand Proverbs 23:7 as saying that as a person thinks in the center of his or her being, so is that person. Or, as in Romans 12:2, we are transformed by having the center of our being renewed. If we know what needs to be renewed, we're one step closer to experiencing real transformation.

In the last twenty years, those who study the brain have confirmed much of what Scripture has been telling us all along.

Some of these discoveries have helped to explain why it is so hard to transform, or renew, our minds. They've also identified why some of our sinful patterns are so hard to change, even when we're desperate to change them. The Bible describes how we, by faith, come into a relationship with God through Jesus Christ, and then it also refers to a continual process of being transformed by the Holy Spirit of God. Much of that process has become clearer as a result of the insights we now have into how the brain works. Two major problems in the way we think have been identified.

Our Negative Bias

Jerry is a salesman who has successfully survived the economic downturn, but to talk with him, you'd think he was a total failure. All he can see are the potential problems. He just knows his latest sale will fall through for some reason or other, and there won't be any commission check at the end of the month. He is so negative about everything that his co-workers have labeled him "the eternal pessimist." His response is to say that he is only being a realist. "After all," he argues, "deals do fall apart at the last minute." He will quickly remind people that three months ago he had two deals fall apart at the last minute. One year, he was so certain a deal would close that he even spent part of the commission check he expected to get, only to have to return what he bought because there was no commission check. He said he learned an important lesson that year—don't trust any deal until it is completed and shipped and payment has been received! He is convinced that his "realistic pessimism" works.

Jerry illustrates the first problem we encounter when we want to be transformed by the renewing of our minds. The truth is we all have a natural proclivity to the negative. In fact, we're hardwired to focus on it! The brain is like Velcro when it comes to a negative experience, and it is like Teflon when it comes to a positive experience. This is true for even the most optimistic person. In the next chapter we'll look more closely at what we are learning about how the brain works, but for now know that there are basically three systems in the brain. The first system seeks to avoid danger and harm; the second system approaches situations looking for reward; and the third system, which we will look at in chapter 7, forms attachments and connections with other people.

The system that seeks to avoid danger and harm has been called the "fight-or-flight response." When we are threatened by something dangerous or harmful, our brain prepares our body to either fight against the danger or take flight from the danger. Blood is taken from the brain and sent to our extremities—arms and legs—to prepare us to fight or run. These dangerous circumstances always have a sense of urgency about them. If we are confronted by a dangerous or harmful situation, we must deal with it quickly, for our survival as human beings depends on our vigilance and preparation. So we are perpetually on guard against danger or harm.

In days gone by, our ancestors faced dangers different than the ones we face today. Some of them may have lived through the Great Depression, barely being able to survive. Other ancestors may have faced physical danger as their wagon train moved west. Some of us have faced bullies in school or other situations that we experienced as potentially harmful. We have all, at some time or other, experienced a fight-or-flight situation. While you might now be tempted to dismiss some of these situations you experienced as a child, just remember how fearful or how aggressive you were in those situations.

Think back to the last thing you thought about as you went to sleep last night. Most of us think about some negative thing we faced during the day, or some negative things we might possibly face the next day. If we experienced, say, twenty situations in a day, and ten of those situations were positive, nine were neutral events, and only one was negative, we'd inevitably dwell on the single negative experience!

We're also quicker to show negative emotions on our face than we are to show positive emotions. Those who study the emotional language of the face can detect a split-second expression of anger. The look quickly washes over our faces and disappears in a flash. Even though the expression might be there for only a microsecond, scientists can show it to us on video.

And the final reason we so easily get tangled up in the negative is that we learn things much faster when we experience pain than when we experience pleasure. Painful experiences imprint more deeply on our brain than do positive experiences. We all struggle with this tendency to the negative, and our mind will take the shape of whatever we put in it. So when we ruminate, worry, feel resentment, feel we've been treated unfairly, or have any other negative response, we're downloading the negative and we end up hardwired to focus on it.

The Powerlessness of Our Willpower

Jessica struggled for years with panic attacks. She was determined they would not impact her day-by-day behavior. When she felt her anxiety starting to rise, she would brace herself and will herself not to panic, usually to no avail. The panic would eventually win the battle over her will, and she would end up powerless and in the grip of a frightening panic attack.

Jessica was face-to-face with the second system at work that can block the renewing of our minds. She found that she really was powerless when it came to her willpower. Though we know it's true, we hate to admit it. Think back to your last diet. How long did it last? And what about your commitment to keep that weight off? How long did that last? Our willpower runs out of energy and lets us down. Why is that? It's because we really have two minds that can be at war with each other! Paul describes this battle in Romans 7: "I want to do what is right, but I can't. I want to do what is good, but I don't. I don't want to do what is wrong, but I do it anyway" (vv. 18–19). Paul calls one mind "the sinful nature," or the flesh, and the other he calls "God's good commands." Here we'll say that the part of the mind that wills the good is called the conscious mind, and the part of the mind we can't control is called the subconscious mind.

Many of us recoil at the idea of the subconscious, for somehow along the way we picked up the Freudian *interpretation* of the subconscious. We may feel scared because we think of the subconscious as some powerful, dark, evil part of our mind that is obsessed with sex. Thankfully, that's not what I'm talking about at all. In fact, in this discussion about the subconscious, those ideas are totally meaningless! What brain scientists call the subconscious mind is very different. It is a very safe and understandable part of our mind. Without emotion, it is simply the database of our stored experiences, those things we experienced very early in our life. In fact, we can think of the subconscious mind as being similar to the hard drive on a computer. The hard drive contains all the programs that make the computer work, and our subconscious mind is what makes a large part of our life work the way it does. This early programming of our subconscious mind directs most of our behavior.

We've all had the experience of getting caught up in a conversation with someone while we are driving. For miles, our conscious mind carries on this enjoyable conversation. While this is happening, what is our subconscious mind doing? It's doing the driving. And our subconscious mind does a very good job of driving, for we arrive at our destination safely even though our conscious mind hardly noticed that we were driving the car. Our conscious mind only handles about 5 percent of what goes on in our daily lives, while the subconscious mind handles the other 95 percent of what goes on.

In addition, our subconscious mind is incredibly quick. It makes our conscious mind seem lethargic and slow in comparison. In fact, our subconscious mind can process internal and environmental stimuli at the rate of 20,000,000 per second! That's right—twenty million! That's incomprehensible. Our subconscious mind constantly scans and observes the internal and external stimuli all around and within us. In contrast, the conscious mind can process environmental stimuli at the rate of only forty per second. It's clear which part of our mind is more powerful.

Our conscious mind is also slower than the subconscious mind. It takes the conscious mind between five hundred and six hundred milliseconds to experience something. That means that everything that we experience happening has already happened between five hundred and six hundred milliseconds ago. But the subconscious mind registers these experiences in less than fifty milliseconds. So by the time we are consciously aware of something happening, our subconscious mind has already been processing it.[1]

An important difference between these two minds is that the conscious mind is the "self" that we are. Who we are and how we see ourselves is a product of the conscious mind. It also has the ability to be aware of events in the past as well as ones we anticipate in the future, whereas the subconscious mind learns from the past and is based on past experience but only deals with the present. It is always "on duty" in our here and now. And the subconscious has no awareness of the self, of who we are.

Ever have someone "push your buttons"? All of those buttons that other people push are in our subconscious. And since the subconscious processes so quickly, when someone pushes one of our buttons, we often react before we even think.

For example, Bruce Lipton tells of his first experience with kinesiology—a chiropractor was testing his muscle strength. He was told to hold out his arm and to resist the downward pressure the chiropractor would put on his arm. He was able to resist easily. Then he was asked to say, "My name is Bruce," while the pressure was applied to his arm. Again, he resisted easily. When he was asked to say, "My name is Mary," he says his "arm sunk like a stone."[2]

Of course, he thought it was due to not being ready, so he asked to do it again. As he said, "My name is Mary," his arm was again powerless to resist the pressure. The chiropractor explained that when his conscious mind encountered a belief that was against something he knew to be true—something held as truth in the subconscious mind—the conflict would express itself in a weakening of the body's muscles.[3] That's how powerful our subconscious mind is.

In a very real sense, it is the subconscious mind that is running most of the activities in our lives. So what happens when the conscious mind wants to do something, but the subconscious mind doesn't want to? Eventually, the subconscious mind will win the battle. That's why willpower only works for a short time. What we are "willing" to take place is often at odds with what is programmed into our subconscious.

Look again at the example of wanting to lose weight. We go on a diet. We are determined. Our conscious mind has made the commitment. But our subconscious mind was programmed to see food as an emotional reward. When we were good, or when someone hurt our feelings, our mother made special cookies for us, and we would sit and eat them and talk with Mom. So our conscious mind says "lose weight," but our subconscious mind remembers the warm feelings we had with cookies, milk, and Mom. Eventually the subconscious wears down the conscious mind and our diet simply fails. The subconscious has won the battle.

Typically, by the time we are six years old or so, the programming of our subconscious mind is pretty much completed. The hard drive appears to be full. It is programmed by what we saw our parents doing, by what they and other adults were saying to us, and by other early experiences. For example, if during this period of our life a parent was often angry with us and called us "stupid," that got programmed into our subconscious mind. Later, in adulthood, we may often be haunted by the sense that we are stupid. Until we deal with it, it will be part of our program.

That program also includes things like how our parents played with us or disciplined us. All kinds of words and looks and behaviors we saw in them became a part of our hard drive. In addition, traumatic experiences that happened during later stages of life also get programmed into our subconscious.[4]

Think back to the last time someone said something to you that really caused you to react negatively. When they pushed your button, what were you really reacting to? As you look back on it, you may be embarrassed by the intensity of your reaction. If you think back as far as you can to identify similar feelings related to that experience, in almost every case your "button" will take you back to something hurtful that happened to you, or something painful you saw or experienced, prior to age six.

The power of our subconscious mind is why simply using positive thinking doesn't always work the way we think it should. It's why we can only maintain the change for a short time. When we are trying to change our thoughts or behaviors without factoring in the impact of our subconscious mind, our conscious mind will *always* lose the battle. What we most need is something that will change the programming of our hard drive!

When our conscious mind and our subconscious mind are in sync with each other, we're finally working with all cylinders firing. When this happens, unlike when our beliefs are in conflict with those imbedded in our subconscious mind, our beliefs at last have great power. It also explains why, when we read the Bible, we may skip over the parts that are in conflict with what we believe in our subconscious mind and unwittingly search for what is consistent with the beliefs of our subconscious.

I recently spoke with a man who was very angry with God. Unable to find God, he said he felt like David must have felt when he was running away from King Saul. Though I tried to get him to see that it was okay for him to be angry with God, he would agree for a moment and then negate anything I had said. I finally suggested he read through the Psalms to see how David reacted when he was angry and disappointed with God.

I wanted this man to see that even when David expressed his anger and frustration, he ultimately affirmed his faith and trust in God. I wanted him to see that he could be angry with God while remaining in relationship. Though rising to the challenge, working through all the Psalms, the man still didn't get the point. Instead, he focused on Psalm 88, the *one Psalm* where the writer did not end with an affirmation of God's faithfulness! That Psalm matched the beliefs of his subconscious: if he was angry, he was bad and God would reject him. He failed to take in the message of the overwhelming number of other Psalms that affirmed what I had wanted him to see. In the end, they made little impact on his thinking.

For any one of us, though, there are plenty of things we believe that aren't necessarily in conflict with our subconscious. One example is the power of what is called the *placebo effect*. A placebo is a fake medication that a patient believes to be real. It might be used as a control when a new medication is first being tested. In these studies, one group takes the new medication, and the other group, unaware they're *not* on the new medication, takes a sugar pill, a placebo. To the frustration of the pharmaceutical companies, about 55 to 60 percent of those taking the placebo will experience the same changes that are supposed to come only from taking the actual medication. They experience real change because of the power of their beliefs. Though pharmaceutical companies would prefer to eliminate from testing those who might respond to a placebo—an impossible agenda—it might be more interesting, though less profitable, if they discovered instead why a placebo can be almost as effective as the real medication!

Another example of the power of belief is illustrated in a number of commonly reported studies. For example, a teacher is told that several kids in his or her classroom, who are really average, are identified as being brilliant. In one case in which three students were identified as brilliant, the teacher was told she was going to be monitored to make certain she gave no special attention to those three children. And although the monitors had trouble identifying exactly what had changed, the teacher's confidence in those three children was nonetheless communicated. Each of the three identified students not only outperformed the rest of their class, they also continued to do so in their subsequent years of schooling. Past records of these three students confirmed that they were not brilliant, just average. But the belief of the teacher was communicated in such a way that the children responded positively.[5] The placebo effect relates to something positive happening that isn't supposed to happen, given the circumstances.[6]

The opposite of the placebo effect is what is called the *nocebo effect*, a negative belief that also has power. Think what happens when a doctor tells a cancer patient that he has six months to live, or lets a woman know that due to her genetic makeup she will most likely develop breast cancer. Because a doctor is seen as an authority, people will often believe what they are being told. One man was told by his doctor that he had a severe form of cancer and had only a couple of weeks to live. He died several weeks later. But when the autopsy was done, the medical examiner could not find any of the cancer that was supposed to have killed him. The doctor had been mistaken in his diagnosis. What an incredible example of the power of negative beliefs![7]

Another study on the power of beliefs was done by a surgeon who specialized in knee surgery. He got permission to do an experiment in which he studied three groups of people suffering severe disabilities related to their knees, all of whom were in great pain. Most of them needed a cane to walk, and none of them were able to do any exercise that required the use of their legs. Those in one group were given the full surgical treatment on their knees, a complete knee replacement procedure. Following surgery, they improved as expected. The second group had only minor surgery, their knees being only cleaned out of any irritants. Following surgery, they improved the same as the first group. The third group was given "fake surgery." The doctor made the incision but did nothing to the knee. Not knowing exactly what a person remembered while under anesthesia, he pretended to go through the whole process as if he was doing a full surgery on the knee. Amazingly, everyone in this group saw the same improvement as those in the other two groups. Each group believed they'd had the full surgery treatment.[8]

This third group wasn't told about the fake surgery until two years later. At that point, everyone in that group was functioning well. When told he had been given fake surgery, one man in this group, who was now playing basketball, simply said, "Well, miracles do happen." In the follow-up two years later, no difference was found between the groups in what the individuals experienced and how they improved. Yet another amazing example of the power of belief in what an authority figure tells us that is consistent with the beliefs of our subconscious mind.

Can we be transformed by the renewing of our mind, the center of our being? Can we overcome our negative bias?

Can we effectively in some way reprogram our subconscious mind? What about my vow? Could I become the father to my sons that my father never was to me? It seems as though Paul is saying that transformation is a cooperative effort between us and God when he says, "Work hard to show the results of your salvation, obeying God with deep reverence and fear. For God is working in you, giving you the desire and the power to do what pleases him" (Phil. 2:12–13). Let's examine what actually goes on in the brain when we cooperate with God in this process of being transformed.

2

The Physiology of Change

In 1969, an article was published in a science journal accompanied by a photo of a weird-looking machine. It was a picture of an old dentist chair that had been modified to include rows of vibrators on the seat back, along with lots of wires that connected these vibrators to a large computer. (Of course, all computers were large at that time.) The experiment involved having a person who had been blind since birth sit in the chair with his bare back against the row of vibrators. In front of him was a large television camera that he could move around. In the computer, the images from the camera were modified to pixels, much like what a digital camera does today, except, of course, they were in black and white. These images were sent from the camera to the computer and translated into electrical signals, and then were sent to the rows of vibrators against the man's back.

Gradually the test subject would begin to experience what the chair was designed to accomplish. And when he did, the results were totally amazing! Six different subjects were able for the first time to actually see. They did not see anything through their eyes—remember, they were blind from birth. They saw through the patterns of vibrations that stimulated their back! Eventually, through this device, they were able to learn to read and to identify the faces of those in the room, along with their facial expressions. They could tell which objects were closer to them and which were farther away.

Later, as part of the experiment, a ball was thrown to the blind person from in front of them and the camera, and the person in the chair would duck appropriately. If the camera was pointed to the area behind him and the ball was thrown from behind, he would duck in a way that showed he knew where the ball was coming from.

With training, each person's brain was able to translate the electrical stimulations on their backs into vision. The part of the brain that handled vision was intact—it was the optic nerve that connected the retina with the brain that didn't work. That's why these men born blind were able to see through their back. This was one of the early studies that showed that even in adults, the brain can be trained to do amazing things.[1]

Erik Weihenmayer is a blind rock climber who sees through his tongue. He also climbs mountains. In 2001, he was the first blind climber to reach the summit of Mount Everest. Rather than having light hit his retina and send electrical impulses that his brain translates into images, Erik has a device called a BrainPort that delivers these same impulses through his tongue, which are then translated into images in his brain. *Discover* magazine reported on this and pointed out how sensitive the tongue is—equipped with the BrainPort, it can discriminate two points that are spaced less than a millimeter apart.[2] The device was created by Paul Bach-y-Rita, the same man who helped the blind men see through their back. So Erik can play soccer with his daughter and compete in a game of tic-tac-toe.

Why should we be surprised? King David told us that God "made all the delicate, inner parts of my body and knit me together in my mother's womb. Thank you for making me so wonderfully complex! Your workmanship is marvelous—how well I know it" (Ps. 139:13–14). If we really take what he said literally, we'll see that our brain's ability to adapt is just another part of God's amazing creation. And the part of us that is the most complex is the brain.

An Overview of the Brain

In the last twenty years, knowledge about how the brain functions has exploded. The more we learn, the more amazed we are at the brain's complexity. One can think of the brain as being like an overgrown jungle. It is made up of over one hundred billion brain cells. These brain cells are called *nerve cells*, or *neurons*. If we took one of these brain cells out and examined it, we would find that it has a body that contains genetic information, as well as some other parts that generate energy. This part of the cell is called the nucleus. Then we would see that there are two other parts that extend out from the cell and are in contact with the appropriate parts of other cells. One of these parts is called the *axon*. Each cell has only one axon, and each axon has up to ten thousand "fingers" at its end that point away from the body of the cell. The axon uses these fingers to connect to other neurons. The axon can be long, extending from our brain all the way out to our toes or fingertips. Its task is to send out information to other cells. It is the teaching part of the cell. The axon is covered with a sheath, called the *myelin sheath*, which is like a sleeve that covers a person's arm. This sheath insulates the axon and allows it to pass along its information more quickly.

Extending out along the other sides of the cell nucleus are the *dendrites*. These dendrites receive information from an axon connected to another cell. Dendrites can extend out from the cell in all directions except to where the axon is extended. Each cell can have anywhere from one to ten thousand dendrites. The dendrites' task is that of a learner, receiving the information being sent out by the "teacher," the axon of another cell. Dendrites are always gathering information and passing it back to the axon, which sends it out to the other brain cells with which it is communicating.

If we think of the multiplicity of ways the one hundred billion brain cells can communicate with each other through the dendrites, we will end up with over one thousand trillion possible connections between the cells in our brain. These connections are constantly changing, which leads to the fact that there are more ways for our brain cells to communicate with each other than there are atoms in the universe. When David wrote Psalm 139, he had no idea as to how complex we really are or how marvelous God's workmanship is in knitting each of us together! Yet at some level he was in awe simply because he knew the Creator.

How Do the Cells Communicate?

While you are reading this paragraph, your brain cells are communicating with each other and changing their connective patterns to accommodate what you are reading. How do they communicate with each other? At the end of each axon and each dendrite are communication channels called *synapses*. These are extremely tiny spaces between a dendrite's fingerlike end and an axon's fingerlike end. The size of a synapse is hard to imagine. You know how long a millimeter is, so try to imagine a space that is twenty millionths of a millimeter. That's the size of a synapse!

Each synapse is filled with what are called *neurotransmitter substances*. These are the chemicals that transfer information across the synapse between the axon and the dendrite. One of them is called *serotonin*. You've probably heard of serotonin, because television commercials for antidepressive or sleep medications refer to it. You may also have heard about another substance called *dopamine*. These are only two of the more than fifty known neurotransmitter substances that are in that tiny synapse between an axon and a dendrite in our brain. When a cell wants to communicate with another brain cell, it sends an electrical impulse from the axon down to the fingerlike end of the axon where the synapse is attached. When the electrical impulse reaches the synapse, it is transformed into one of the chemical transmitter substances and sent across the synapse. On the other side of the synapse in the fingerlike part of a dendrite are sites called *receptors* that are waiting for the transfer of the chemical substance. Once the chemical information crosses the synapse to the specialized receptor on the dendrite, it is transformed back again into an electrical impulse and sent up the axon of that cell to the nucleus.

Not only are there over fifty known transmitter substances, but the intensity of the chemical neurotransmitter substance can also vary from strong to weak, which makes the number of possible electrochemical interactions in the brain beyond comprehension. And to know that this is what is going on all through our brain constantly is way beyond what we can imagine.

When Paul says "we are God's masterpiece" (Eph. 2:10), those of us who know God as our Creator simply stand in awe at his craftsmanship. It takes more faith to believe that all of this just happened by chance than to believe there is a master designer who created us with all of these intricate parts and processes. Maybe someday we will discover how an electrical impulse can change into a chemical and then back into an electrical impulse, and how our brain can do that countless times during the microsecond our mind is actually learning something, or saying something, or simply having a thought.

The neuroscientists tell us that brain cells that fire together, wire together. We could also say that the more certain brain cells "talk" to certain other brain cells, the more they like to talk to each other. They form a relationship together. Because of this wiring together, some of our patterns of thinking and behaving are predictable. But because our cells are constantly making new connections, there are many other new and fresh patterns that are possible. Talk about a complex creation.

However, when it comes to reprogramming our hard drive—our subconscious—we have to break apart some of these hardwired communication patterns between certain brain cells in order to create and establish new transforming patterns that will get wired into our brain.

The Triune Brain

To help us understand more how the brain works and what we can do to transform our thoughts, we can divide the brain into three parts. At the core of our brain is what is often called the *primitive* part. This is the part of the brain that is found in every other living creature. We are never aware consciously of what this part of our brain is doing. It just does what it is designed to do all on its own.

In the primitive brain there are basically two parts. One part is called the *brain stem*, which sits at the top of the spinal cord and extends up into the heart of the brain. It is about the size of a person's little finger, and it is what keeps us alive. It handles our breathing and maintains our heart rate and blood pressure. It also tells us when we need to go to sleep and when we need to wake up.

The other part of the primitive brain is called the *cerebellum*, and it is located at the back of the brain. One of its primary tasks is to give us our sense of balance. It is also involved in initiating the fight-or-flight response when we are faced with impending harm or danger. The cerebellum coordinates the movement of the various parts of our body as well. It manages the muscles we use when we do a simple thing like walking. It controls our fine muscles that allow us to do things like write or play the piano. Current research is finding that this core part of the brain regulates to some degree our emotions.[3] The activities of this part of the brain are impacted by conscious efforts that will all become unconscious actions without any input from the other parts of the brain, or from us directly. An example of a conscious action becoming unconscious would be learning to walk. As toddlers begin to walk, they are focusing on the actions needed in order to walk. Quickly their brain learns how to connect all the actions that make up walking, and they never consciously think they have to put one foot in front of the other.

The second part of the triune brain is a small bundle of parts located within the brain just above the brain stem called the *limbic system*. Like the primitive brain, it operates outside of our conscious awareness. The limbic system is responsible for many things, including recognizing and remembering experiences, especially fearful ones. It is the center of our emotions and is highly connected to our conscious brain. It will initiate and communicate to the conscious brain our experiences of fear, joy, disgust, anger, hurt, and countless other emotions. It is also the motivational center in our brain. It is like an in-between part of the brain that is highly connected to, and communicates with, the primitive brain as well as the conscious part of the brain (discussed below).

Included in the limbic system are a number of different little parts. One is called the *thalamus*, which receives and processes what is going on in the world around us. It's like a relay station in our brain. For example, it sends information to another part of the limbic system called the *basal ganglia*. This information will direct our body movements, perhaps causing us to move our bodies away from a dangerous situation if it seems necessary. Its decision about moving is based on what the thalamus is picking up from the outside world.

Another part of the limbic system is called the *hypothalamus*. It differs from the thalamus in that instead of monitoring the external world around us, it is monitoring our internal world, regulating how much we eat or drink, keeping our body temperature stable, and regulating our hormones. It is one of the busiest parts of the limbic system as it seeks to maintain stability in all of our bodily functions. It is also the part of the brain that communicates with the pituitary gland, which regulates the release of hormones into our blood. It's amazing how these little parts of the brain work together without our having any awareness of what they are doing!

A third part of the limbic system is peanut shaped and is called the *hippocampus*. This is a very important part of the brain that we will consider more carefully later in the chapter, as it is highly connected to our ability to be transformed by the renewing of our mind. The hippocampus is a key to how God designed us to make this transformation possible. It handles our short-term memory, deciding what needs to be sent to the third part of our triune brain—the conscious part—where it becomes a part of our long-term memory. The hippocampus is also highly related to learning new things.

The *cingulate cortex* is another part of the limbic system, and its task is to evaluate and rank the importance of what is going on inside and outside of our bodies. It helps us to know what needs closer attention. It monitors our plans, helping us to integrate thinking and feeling together. It is also our worry center.

The *nucleus accumbens* is a small part of the limbic system, but it is an important part of the pleasure centers in the brain. It also serves as a storage center for the neurotransmitter substance dopamine.

Another important part of the limbic system is the *amygdala*, which is the core of our warning system. It operates as our alarm. It will warn us of pending danger from things that are emotionally charged, are potentially dangerous, or could have a negative effect on our well-being.

And finally, there is our pituitary gland. Based on signals from the other parts of the limbic system, it will release into our system calming chemicals like endorphins or oxytocin. It will also, when told to do so, release stress hormones, including histamines, adrenaline, and cortisol, which are designed in part to prepare us to either take flight or stand and fight against a possible threat.

Lastly, we come to the third part of the triune brain, called the *neocortex*. This is the conscious part of our brain that allows us to reason and regulate our emotions. This part makes up the "thinking" brain. The neocortex is the wrinkled, spongelike layer that covers the other two parts of the triune brain. It is what we see when we look at a model of the whole brain. Since it is basically gray in color, it is the reason we sometimes refer to our brain as *gray matter*. The neocortex deals with complex thinking, including abstract and creative thinking. It manages our language skills along with our sensory and motor abilities. The major part of the neocortex is called the *prefrontal cortex*, which is in the front of the brain and rests just behind our forehead. The prefrontal cortex is the part that makes us aware of who we are, makes decisions, and has to do with motivation and finding meaning in what we think or do. It makes us uniquely human and is often called the executive part of our brain.

This is an overview of the basic parts of the brain, which is so much more involved and far more complex than what I've described. We also need to remember that our brain extends itself via our nerves to all the other organs and various parts of our body.

What Happens in Our Brain

In order to better understand what we've been describing, let's look at what happens in our brain when we experience three different things: when we are afraid, when we are stressed, and when we are depressed.

When We Are Afraid

Fear, when experienced in the here and now, is a healthy emotion that everyone faces. It plays a major part in protecting us, and it is one of the primary emotions we all feel at some time or another. For an example of healthy fear, let's imagine a situation in which you are hiking. As you round a bend in the trail, you see what looks like a snake up ahead on the path. It even looks like a picture you've seen of a very poisonous snake. You stop in your tracks. What happens in your brain? Immediately your optic nerve sends an image to your brain, and at the same time a signal is sent to the amygdala, the warning center in your brain. Instantly the amygdala shouts, "Emergency!" or "Danger! Danger!" This warning activates your autonomic nervous system, causing your heart rate to increase and your blood pressure to rise, all designed to get you ready to react. In addition, blood is being taken away from your organs and your digestive system. It is being sent to your arms and legs to prepare you to either attack the snake or run away—to fight or take flight.

At the same time, the hypothalamus sends a message to the pituitary gland to release adrenaline into your bloodstream. All this will occur within a microsecond, and before you can finish reading this sentence, you would have in all probability made the decision to turn and run. Sometimes in this kind of situation, you may freeze in place, which is also a fear response. But your first reaction will usually be to get away from the danger. If you've had close encounters with dangerous snakes before, or if you are deathly afraid of snakes in general, your reaction will be even quicker and stronger.

We have a slower version of the alarm system built into our brain as well, and it is operating at the same time as the above described fast version. As our amygdala is first sounding the alarm, the optic nerve is also sending the information to our thalamus, which sends the information to the prefrontal cortex for evaluation. *Is it really a snake?* Our prefrontal cortex—the thinking part of the brain—evaluates what it sees and, using reason, decides that what we see is a tree limb and not a snake. Our prefrontal cortex will overrule the first danger signal and send an all-clear signal to the amygdala, causing the process to stop and reverse itself. Your heart rate will return to normal, as will your blood pressure. The blood will be sent from the extremities back to the digestive system and the other organs. The stress hormones like cortisol that were released will stay in your system, and it will take a good night's sleep or some exercise to get them out of your system. It's hard for us to imagine that this very complex process goes on every time we face a real or potential danger.

Today, most of us don't have very many acute fearful situations like meeting a deadly snake on a trail. But many of us still live chronically fear-based lives, and it doesn't take much to get the fear cycle going in our brain and in our body. We live in a state of hypervigilance where the pituitary gland is constantly releasing adrenaline, histamines, and cortisol into our system. The cousins of fear—anxiety and worry—set off the same physiological process in our brain and then in our body. So if we are anxious a lot or worry a lot, the same flow of stress hormones is being released into our system that would have been released when we thought we were seeing a deadly snake.

Our bodies were not designed by God to have this process continually activated. When we live with a constant feeling of dread or anxiety or worry, we are releasing the stress hormones into our body to the point at which they build up in our system. When they build up at a continual rate, they eventually compromise our health and greatly limit our ability to renew our minds.

When this fear cycle is set off and adrenaline and the other stress hormones are released into our system, their presence gradually shuts down our immune system. The immune system and the adrenal system will not work at the same time. For example, let's say you are suffering from a bad case of the flu and are bedridden to fight off a fever and the chills. Suddenly someone yells through your front door that your house is on fire. Your brain must make a decision—does it continue to work on conquering the flu, or does it mobilize your body to get up out of bed and out of the house? The choice is obvious. You will find the ability to get out of that bed and out of the burning house! Your body will deal with the flu later. The adrenal system always overrules the immune system.

What this means is that when we live a fear-based lifestyle, feeling anxious and worried most of the time, we are continually activating our adrenal system. The more we live this way, the more our thoughts are filled with anxiety and worries—it is a deadly cycle. The result is an immune system that cannot operate as it was designed to, and our health will always suffer.

When We Are Stressed

Stress is the natural consequence of living a life struggling with fear, worry, and anxiety. Not everyone lives a fear-based lifestyle, but they may still struggle with continual stress. We live in a stress-filled world, and it is difficult to escape from the stress of everyday life. Our bodies are not built for the 24-7 level of stress so many of us experience. We have the stress of juggling the pressures of work, of finances and paying the bills, of the needs and demands of our kids, of family issues, and of interrupting phone calls. Then on top of all that is the stress created by the information overload to which we are all exposed. Eventually stress will wear us down and make us vulnerable to all kinds of physical and emotional problems. I talk with people whose doctor has told them that their adrenal system doesn't work anymore. It's just plain worn out. Their chronic stress from dealing with life has taken that toll on them.

When our lives are filled with fear, worry, and anxiety over a period of time, or we are living an overwhelmingly stressful life, several things will eventually happen to us. The parts of our brain that handle memory and learning—in particular, the hippocampus—will age more quickly. An aging hippocampus means it is shrinking in size. When it does, our memory begins to fade and our brain slows down. Histamines are released, which causes inflammation that works against a healthy mind and body. Cortisol, the stress hormone, builds up in our system, causing us to struggle with sleeplessness and fatigue—all of which are detrimental to our health.

One researcher described the effects of chronic stress this way. Imagine runners getting ready for a race. When they hear the judge say, "On your mark!" they get in place for the start of the race. When the judge says, "Get set," they tense every muscle in their bodies as they prepare for the releasing command. When the judge fires the starter's pistol or says, "Go," the runners explode out of the starting block and expend every bit of energy to run the race. But what happens if there is no "go" signal given? The runners are left at the starting blocks, their blood coursing with adrenaline, their bodies fatiguing with the strain of preparing for a race that never comes. Despite their excellent physical condition, within a short period of time they would quickly all collapse there on the starting line from the strain of staying in that "get set" position.[4]

The problem is that today we live in a "get set" world. We are like the runners in the blocks waiting, but no "go" signal is ever given. Our worries and anxieties never let up, and the stress on our bodies makes our immune systems so weak that the majority of all major illnesses can be linked to chronic stress.

This is not the way God meant for us to live. Paul tells us that when we renew our minds and center our thoughts on the right things, we "will experience God's peace, which exceeds anything we can understand" (Phil. 4:7). What a promise! We can experience God's peace in the midst of our "get set" world. In fact, we are all designed by God to experience his peace!

When We Are Depressed

For years, depression has been defined as a chemical imbalance in the brain. There is a shortage of transmitter substances in the synapse, causing our brain to slow down, almost as if the brain's "batteries" are weak. The latest medicines prescribed for depression work on building up serotonin in the synapses of the brain. They are called selective serotonin reuptake inhibitors (SSRIs). They work by blocking the receptors on the dendrite from absorbing the serotonin that is present, so the quantity of serotonin in the synapse will increase—sort of like having the batteries recharged. They have provided an effective treatment for a lot of people.

Current research, however, is increasingly suggesting that most depression does not begin as a chemical imbalance in the brain that affects the brain's ability to produce serotonin, or dopamine in particular. What they are finding is that most depression is caused by the effects of chronic stress, which has shrunk both the hippocampus and the prefrontal cortex—the executive part of the brain. Depression is the result of stress hormones, such as adrenaline and cortisol, inhibiting the growth of these two important parts of the brain in the same way fear, anxiety, worry, and stress would.[5] It's as if the effect of aging—that is, the shrinking of the hippocampus—is accelerated by the increased presence of the stress hormones.

One of the symptoms of depression is an inability to get the right kind of sleep. When we are dealing with the stress hormones in our system, sleep deprivation adds to an already destructive cycle in the brain. The levels of our stress hormones are designed to drop while we sleep. When we don't get enough sleep, the levels continue to build. They continue to pile up in our system while all the time working against our physical and emotional health. Whenever our hippocampus and our prefrontal cortex are shrinking, transformation—the change we want to make in our lives—is very difficult. But God knew what he was doing when he created our brain. He gives us a solution when we choose to walk his path.

Summary

What are we to do? We've all tried to reduce the amount of stress in our lives, but how does one really do that in our rapid-paced world? We have all made vows to change, only to break them and end up feeling frustrated and hopeless. But God wouldn't offer the possibility of a transformed life if there was no solution, no way we could break the cycle. What is amazing to me is that those who are doing all this fresh research on the brain have found an answer. They all agree that there are three things that anyone can do to transform their way of thinking and living. The first they point to is the importance of physical exercise. They are quick to say that one doesn't have to train like an athlete to get the benefit of exercise. Just walking briskly for twenty to thirty minutes three or four times a week will work wonders in our brain.

Secondly, they have found that novel learning experiences will cause the hippocampus in the brain to grow, which fosters good brain health. Things like learning a new language or some other new area of knowledge will make a big difference in how healthy our brain will be. Taking up something new, like learning to paint or doing stained glass, will work too. New learning experiences cause the hippocampus to grow and to change our brain. The amazing thing is that when we experience transformation, we will have a growing and healthy hippocampus and prefrontal cortex.

But here's where I want to turn our focus. The third thing researchers suggest that will keep our brain young and our bodies healthier is that we must learn how to focus our attention. We live in what some people call the *People* magazine age—we all have short attention spans. If an article in a magazine is more than two pages long, we won't read it all. As a result, we are poor listeners, and our minds wander if they are not stimulated constantly.

This lack of being able to focus our attention works against our brain's health and our being able to renew our minds. God has a plan to help us focus our attention. It's described in Psalm 119, especially in verse 11, which says, "I have hidden your word in my heart, that I might not sin against you." If we want to be transformed by the renewing of our minds, God says not only do we need to hide his Word in the center of our being, but we need to focus our attention on it by pondering it and allowing it to dwell deep within our minds. The key to change is that transformation comes when we get God's words in our minds and we ponder them—we think about them throughout the day. In the next chapter, we'll begin to look at how we can do this.

3

The ABCs of a Renewed Mind

Ellen Langer conducted a fascinating experiment in 1979.[1] Called the *counterclockwise study*, her work involved a group of men who were all seventy-five years old. Researchers wondered what would happen if they ran an experiment designed to turn the mind back twenty years for seven days. Would there be any changes in the body?

The participants were asked to attend a weeklong retreat without being told the purpose of the retreat. Once they arrived, they were told that, for the week, they were going to live as if they were actually only fifty-five years old. They were not allowed to bring anything with them that was dated after 1959. They would watch a black-and-white television, typical of those available in 1959, and the programs and movies they would watch were all from that era. The radio played the musical hits of 1959, magazines and other reading materials were all at least twenty years old, and they discussed the bestsellers published in 1959. Even the retreat center was chosen because it looked ageless. In fact, just a few touches made it look like it was 1959. Each man wore a name tag with a picture of himself when he was fifty-five years old. The men were told that, for the week, they were to talk, think, and act as if it was literally twenty years earlier. All conversations were to include things they remembered from 1959 or earlier.

Prior to the retreat, each man went through a complete series of tests that focused on every aspect of a person that we assume deteriorates with age. Their eyesight was tested. Their memories were tested. They took an IQ test. In addition, a full battery of medical tests was performed, including tests that measured flexibility, hand strength, and even the length of their arthritic fingers. They had photos taken of their faces and videos of their gait and posture. Then for seven days they lived as if it were 1959.

The men had a great time. And when the week was over, all the same tests were run again. The researchers found that the men's memory and eyesight improved by an average of at least 10 percent. Many of their IQ scores were higher. There were also improvements in most of the other tests. Even their arthritic fingers straightened and lengthened. And when photos taken of them before the retreat were compared with ones taken after the retreat, independent evaluators who knew nothing about the nature of the retreat said the men looked three years younger on average.

How did these changes take place? It was the change in their thinking, proving that our biology is not our destiny.

Langer noted, "It is not primarily our physical selves that limit us but rather our mind-set about our physical limits."[2]

The experience of these "younger" older men beautifully illustrates what can happen when we choose to focus our attention in a certain way. They were forced to focus their attention on being fifty-five instead of seventy-five, and it made a difference in all sorts of ways. The surprise to everyone reading this study was that their focus on being fifty-five moved them from feeling their own age physically, emotionally, and mentally toward feeling and really *being* younger!

Focused Attention and the Subconscious Mind

What happens in the brain when something like this is experienced? It's connected to the ways brain cells that fire together, or "talk" together, become wired together. A communication pattern is eventually created in the brain, and the more we use that pattern, the stronger the pattern of thinking becomes.

To better understand this, imagine that you are staying at a cabin in the woods and you decide to go for a walk. Wanting to go where no one else has gone in that part of the woods, you carve out a pathway. Using a machete, you chop branches that block your path. And each day for a week you take a walk on the new path you've created. What was a difficult path to walk the first day becomes easier by the end of the week.

Now imagine that you come back to vacation at the same cabin the next year. When you go to take a walk on "your" path, you find that it is now well worn. Others have walked on the path and smoothed out the way. Now it is an easy walk. All the branches, rocks, and other hindrances that had been in the way the first time you walked that path have been cleared.

In the same way, when brain cells "talk" together over time, a well-worn neural path is created between them, and the thoughts and beliefs these paths represent become a part of our subconscious mind.

Here is an example. Perry did not have a good experience with his mother in his early years. When we talked, he told me about how anytime he did something that upset his mother, she would get angry with him and call him stupid. For instance, there were several times as a small boy that he spilled his glass of milk at the dinner table. And every time he did this, even though it was an accident, his mother would get angry with him and say, "Stupid, can't you do anything right!" He remembers falling down while playing outside and cutting his knee. When he went to his mother for a Band-Aid, she got upset with him and yelled at him for being so careless, as if it was his fault, and that was because he was stupid.

We got into this conversation because as he talked with me, he kept apologizing and referring to himself as being inept or inadequate in some way. I asked him how he knew that he was so worthless, and that's when he explained about his mother. When I asked him how his father reacted to her calling him stupid, he described his father as a very passive and silent man. He went on to tell me that he barely made it through high school, and he didn't go to college because he knew he wasn't smart enough for college. He was working in a low-paying job that he had held for some years, and he had turned down promotions because he was convinced he couldn't do the higher-paying job.

This was part of the programming of his subconscious mind. For as long as he could remember, his mother's favorite word for him was "stupid." His brain cells took in this information, and the first time his mom called him that, it created a pathway in his mind that was weak and probably wouldn't have stayed in his mind if it hadn't been repeated so many times. But each time it was repeated, the thought pattern became stronger until finally it was a major thoroughfare in his brain. Eventually he adopted "stupid," or some similar negative term, as his definition of himself. His image of himself affected everything from his job to his parenting and even his marriage.

On the other hand, consider Trisha. Her experience with her parents as a young child was very different from Perry's. She remembers both of her parents being encouraging and saying to her over and over again, "You can do anything you choose to do. You can do it!" When she wanted to learn to play the piano, the family went out and bought a piano, saying to her, "We know you can do it!" Practicing the piano wasn't an ordeal because her parents enjoyed her playing and encouraged her in her effort. But their encouragement for her to perform left an undeveloped spot in her—she struggled with her personal relationships. She did great with the people who worked for her, but in her personal life, she struggled with what felt to her like a performance trap.

Today Trisha is a very successful businesswoman. She owns a large real estate office and has a number of agents working for her. She enjoys her work and doesn't struggle with feelings of self-doubt. But she's never married. Her work is her life. Her subconscious mind was programmed from an early age to tell her that she was capable and competent, and that if some task was important to her, she would accomplish it. But her parents did not see that a more truthful balance would have been better. In contrast to Perry's, her brain cells had created pathways that created a confident belief system in her ability to perform, not a belief system of being stupid and inadequate.

This is not to say that parents never get it right, but support and reality have to be balanced. The early pathways are powerful.

How Does the Subconscious Do This?

How important are these pathways that develop in our brain? How do they impact us and control us in so many ways? What happened when Perry developed pathways in his brain based on his sense of being stupid, or when Trisha developed pathways in her brain telling her that she could do anything? These pathways form our beliefs about ourselves and about our world. At the deepest level, Perry believed he was incompetent, and that colored everything in his life. Trisha believed she was competent, and that was deeply imbedded in her subconscious mind. For each, it would take only a microsecond to access these beliefs and others like them, and to live out those beliefs that were programmed into their subconscious mind.

Though these pathways are clearly deeply formative, in a typical day we don't pay much attention to the belief systems that are programmed into our subconscious mind. (That's because they are in the subconscious mind!) We are also conditioned to believe that what happens to us is what causes our reactions or responses. For example, if your boss yells at you today and you're in a bad mood the rest of the day, you may be certain that the reason you're in a bad mood is because he yelled at you. What if a driver cuts you off as you're driving home that same evening? You are going to be convinced that the reason you're angry is because of that terrible driver who almost caused a serious accident. With the driver, you may even be plotting revenge. And then later, you go back to thinking that all of your anger was because your boss yelled at you and put you in a bad mood.

We are too easily caught up in that old "stimulus causes response" way of thinking. And when we are in that frame of mind, we give over the control of our lives to our preprogrammed subconscious mind. We don't recognize the real source, so try as we might, we cannot see a way to change.

In reality, there is something that occurs in between the stimulus and the response that causes our reactions and responses. It is our *beliefs*. In my book *You Are What You Think*, I describe this as the ABCs of our emotions and behaviors. *A* refers to an *action*, to something that happens, such as your boss yelling at you or a driver cutting you off on the road and almost causing an accident. *C* refers to the emotional or behavioral *consequences*—our reactions and responses to that action. Your bad mood and your anger, and even your attempt to get even with the other driver, are examples of responses to *A*. What we overlook is that in between *A* and *C* is *B*, which refers to my *beliefs*, and these beliefs create my responses. There are all kinds of optional responses and consequences to a given action based on our current beliefs.

Obviously, there are some days when, as you are driving home, another driver cuts you off. On this day, your response is to simply touch the brakes, slow down a bit, and continue on your way. There's no anger and no thought of getting even with the careless driver. There may even be days when your boss yelled at you but it didn't really bother you, just as the careless driver didn't upset you. The difference is the belief system that is operating at that particular time.

If someone cuts you off on the road and you are having a great day, you hardly notice. You are not upset by that person's bad driving habits. You simply get out of their way and keep singing to the radio. Or if you are having a great day at the office and the boss for some reason is in a terrible mood, when he yells at you, you simply look at your co-worker and you both shrug your shoulders in bewilderment at the boss's behavior. Your beliefs about yourself and about life in those situations are completely different from your beliefs in the earlier examples.

When the boss's yelling at you put you in a bad mood, you were probably already in a place of low self-esteem and had a low-confidence mood. Your belief system at that time was, "The boss is right. I am a terrible employee, and I'm also a terrible person." In contrast, when his yelling at you didn't faze you, your belief system was, "I am a competent person and a worthy employee." In the same way, when the driver cutting you off set off your anger, you were probably feeling entitled to the road. That space on the highway in front of you was yours! You were already in a bad mood and upset. But when that same thing happened on another day and you weren't even fazed by it, your mind was in a great place and you weren't about to let someone else spoil it. It's all tied to your belief system!

Perry's belief system was built around his core belief about himself that he was an incompetent, stupid person. Trisha's belief system was built around her core belief about herself that she could accomplish anything if she put in the effort. These are just two of the many core beliefs that were programmed into their subconscious minds from an early age.

Here's what happens. Each emotion we have causes various hormones to be released in our body through the hypothalamus and the pituitary gland. These hormones are received by the cells and lock into receptors in the cells. These are like drugs that the cells become addicted to. This begins a vicious circle—when I feel an emotion, the hormones are released and satisfy the cells for their "fix."

Now every time this happens, we create links called synapses between specific neurons in our brain. These are the pathways. They become the programming we have created that colors our perceptions and triggers emotions from our past. Changing our reactions and responses means we have to change our perceptions and create new neural pathways in our brain that override the old pathways.

I'm dealing with something similar right now. When I leave my office to go home, I need to make a right turn onto a major street that often has a lot of traffic. But that turn takes me to a special lane for those turning right, and that lane goes a good ways down the major street before it merges. The lane even continues for those who will make a right turn at the next street, as I do. So it seems like it should be easy to make that first right turn. There is no stop sign or even a yield sign at that corner. You are supposed to just move through the turn and then either merge into the traffic going straight or make the next right turn.

As I come out of my office to head home, sometimes there is a line of cars waiting to make a right turn because just one person is sitting there waiting for the traffic on the main street to break. They have the long lane always available for them, but for whatever reason, they hesitate.

The other part of the example is that I have a personal struggle with being impatient. Somehow my impatient neural pathway was established a long time ago, and it's something that has been woven deep within my subconscious mind. I've struggled with it for years, and I have asked God to help me with it. And he is helping me be more patient, except when I come to this corner and someone is just sitting there waiting!

I am beginning to realize that I am impatient with these people because I believe it is incompetent for them to sit there. I used to repeat things to myself such as, "Where did they learn how *not* to drive?" or "If they had any intelligence, they would see the lane and keep moving," or "They must have flunked drivers education!" But now that I am working on being patient, I am fighting those thoughts that represent some of my core beliefs. My progress is evident in that I no longer honk the horn when someone just sits there. But I have also continued to wonder why I can't learn to be more patient in this situation, and to just be more patient in general.

The other morning I was meditating on Ephesians 4, where Paul says, "Always be humble and gentle. Be patient with each other, making allowances for each other's faults because of your love" (v. 2). And of course, I thought about my corner. And then I saw something new as I meditated for a time on that particular verse. Paul coupled together patience with being humble and gentle and acting in love. As I thought about what Paul said, I realized that my impatience was really a form of pride and arrogance. I had never thought of it that way before. I had to ask God for forgiveness for my impatient attitude. It was one of those things I have wanted to change about myself and have worked on, but I had seemed power-less to make any long-term change. I hadn't had a clue as to how my brain had been wired.

But why had I been so powerless about this? Part of it was that I was trying to change my response to the frustrating stimuli without even considering what my belief systems in that situation might be. Now I have seen that my impatience involved pride and arrogance on my part and that God is call-ing me to be humble, gentle, and loving. I am not working on being more patient, I am working on changing my prideful and arrogant belief system. I'm going to tackle head-on my subconscious programming that makes me think that I am the only one who really knows how to drive, especially when it comes to that corner.

Breaking Old Habits

There's another way to look at this process. In his book *The Power of Habit*,[3] Charles Duhigg points out that a *habit*, or what we could call a belief system, has several parts to it. There is always a *cue* that triggers the habit. At the other end is a *reward* associated with the cue. In between the cue and the reward is the habit, or the routine, we follow to reach the reward. And underneath it all is a craving that drives the habit pattern. It's the motivator for the habit.

In my situation just described, my impatience is triggered by my habit of being frustrated. My cue has been to end my day, lock my office, and get in my car. My habit is to smoothly turn the corner from my short side street onto the main road heading for home. My reward is to get home. Underneath all of this is my craving to get home as quickly as possible.

So my habit, or routine, is to typically come out of the office, get in my car, leave the parking lot, and come to that corner. When all goes smoothly, I zip through the corner, head to the next corner, and make another right turn there, and then I'm almost home. That's my habit pattern.

But look at what happens when the corner is blocked by some hesitant drivers. I come to my corner and my habit is blocked—there are two or three cars just sitting there. My craving to get home as quickly as possible is frustrated, and my stress level begins to rise. In the past, I'd blow my horn. Or in my frustration, I would have nasty conversations with these hesitant drivers—of course, only in the privacy of my car. I would even "try" to be patient, but with my elevated stress levels, I would get more frustrated. As I passed one of the hesitant drivers, I'd give him another piece of my mind—all with my window closed, of course.

In situations like this, most people would try to change the cue or the reward—or, most likely, the craving would be the focus. Some people would try to develop patience by changing the habit. I could rid myself of the frustration of that corner by changing my habit and going home a different way, even though it would also be a longer drive. That would be Duhigg's suggestion. But if I do that, I learn nothing about my impatience, nor do I get a chance to develop new patterns of behavior—what Duhigg calls the routine.

So how did I change my behavior? I've not changed the outward habit—I still come to that corner and see it as my desired path home. I've not changed my reward—I still want to zip through the corner and get home. I've not changed my craving—I'm still anxious to get home. What I have changed is my routine, or the internal habit that is my belief system. For example, I now come to the corner and find there are three cars waiting, so I just sit there and consciously relax. I still cheer on those who turn the corner the way it is designed. But I don't belittle those who don't. I tell myself things such as, "Maybe they're intent on getting across traffic to get into the left lane," or "Maybe they don't even see the open lane," or "Maybe they're new around here and not sure of what to do," or "Maybe they're afraid to merge with the oncoming traffic," or "Maybe they're just afraid to venture out into the traffic." I am changing my personal belief system at that corner. In essence, I'm creating a new habit out of my former habit.

What I am also doing is consciously creating new pathways in my brain—new belief systems. And these new routines, or habits, are gradually overtaking the old pathways that I've built over the years in similar situations. It doesn't happen quickly, but the change does come. This is a way to form new habits. And in my case, my old habit, my old routine, is still wired there in my brain, but I have overridden it with new brain pathways. And to keep those pathways growing stronger, I seek to be consistent in how I approach that corner. That may sound like using my willpower, but I am really working on doing it God's way.

There is an even more powerful way to challenge my old beliefs about my impatience in general, and my impatience at that corner specifically. In my meditation on Scripture, I focus my attention on what God is telling me. I need to keep reminding myself to ponder the thought that my impatience is basically a matter of pride and arrogance. And as I am working at hiding God's Word in my heart (see Ps. 119:11), I continue to ponder those words in Ephesians 4:2 that couple impatience with pride and arrogance.

I can transform my old beliefs and be transformed by the renewing of my mind with beliefs based on what God says, not just on how I've been programmed to think. God does have a program for our transformation! In between the cue and the reward is a routine, or habit, that can and should involve my relationship with God and his Word. I've found that knowing about how I create habits does help. But even more important than that is knowing God's pattern and seeking to build that into my life. That's where the power to change really lies. Let's look at how it works.

4

God's Plan for Our Transformation

Jack sat at his desk reading and rereading the email from his sister. The more he read it, the angrier he became. He couldn't believe what she was saying about him. It wasn't just some abstract email that was railing on some national or impersonal issue—it was angry and negative, and it was all directed at him. He couldn't believe how she could think such things about him, let alone say them. He was hurt, but more than hurt—he was angry! And as he reread the email again for what must have been the tenth time, he could barely contain himself. He began to think of all the angry rebuttals he was going to send back to her. At this point, he didn't care what she would think. He was too angry to care.

He pulled his chair up to the computer and hit reply. And then as his fingers were poised over the keys, a passage he had recently meditated on and committed to memory came flooding into his awareness: "Get rid of all bitterness, rage, anger, harsh words, and slander, as well as all types of evil behavior. Instead, be kind to each other, tenderhearted, forgiving one another, just as God through Christ has forgiven you" (Eph. 4:31–32).

He pushed the verses out of his mind. "Not now," he told himself. "I'm justified in my anger, even if it is rage, and she needs to know it! That verse just doesn't apply in this situation!" But as he looked at the computer again, the phrase "be kind to each other, tenderhearted" kept bouncing around in his mind. He knew God was trying to get his attention.

"But Lord," he protested, "you don't understand!" And then that voice in his head said, *Yes, I do understand. Be kind, tenderhearted!* He slowed down this time and asked the Lord, "But how? I can't believe my sister feels this way about me." And in the silence that followed, Jack pushed away from the computer and took a break.

When he returned several hours later, he had taken the time to rethink the whole email and had framed in his mind a totally different response. This time his response was consistent with the Ephesians passage, and he typed out a kind, tenderhearted response that was still an honest reflection of his hurt. Later that day he got a response from his sister with an apology for her impulsive, hurtful email and an explanation of what had been going on in her life. She admitted that she had taken her frustration out on him and deeply regretted her first email. Jack thanked the Lord for the transforming power of that passage in Ephesians and how his obedience to that particular verse had probably strengthened his relationship with his sister.

The conflict between what God wants in our lives and what we want is very old. It goes way back to when Satan decided he didn't want what God wanted. He had bigger ideas, and he wanted what he selfishly desired. As a result, he led a revolt in heaven and ended up being banished from the presence of God, along with his coconspirators:

> There was war in heaven. Michael and his angels fought against the dragon and his angels. And the dragon lost the battle, and he and his angels were forced out of heaven. This great dragon—the ancient serpent called the devil, or Satan, the one deceiving the whole world—was thrown down to the earth with all his angels. (Rev. 12:7–9)

The devil was not only Michael's enemy, he is our enemy as well. Paul said that the devil disguises himself as an angel of light in order to deceive us (see 2 Cor. 11:14), and Peter said that we are to "stay alert! Watch out for your great enemy, the devil. He prowls around like a roaring lion, looking for someone to devour" (1 Peter 5:8). Paul tells us to "put on every piece of God's armor so you will be able to resist the enemy" (Eph. 6:13). The enemy he refers to is the devil. James adds that we are not to turn and run from Satan; we are to "resist the devil, and he will flee from you" (James 4:7).

What happens when we try so desperately to change something in our lives, only to fail time and time again, is that we are caught in this same ageless battle. It is a battle between what God wants in our lives and what our enemy, the devil, wants to accomplish in us. It's like we are in a tug-of-war between God and the devil. We want to change, to be transformed, but we just cannot figure out how to let God accomplish what both he and we desire to change. We even fight against what we know is best for us and then cry out, "Lord, why can't I change?"

Paul described his own personal war as an internal battle against two different ways to live. He described that battle this way: "The trouble is with me, for I am all too human, a slave to sin. I don't really understand myself, for I want to do what is right, but I don't do it. Instead, I do what I hate" (Rom. 7:14–15). His struggle is all too familiar. Why can't we do what we want to do? He didn't know about the subconscious mind specifically, but he certainly knew about the struggle. Today he might describe the conflict as being between the frustrating beliefs programmed into his subconscious mind that were opposed to what God desired for him, and those beliefs that wanted to please God. The challenge of being transformed boils down to the fact that there are two ways to live that are at war with each other, and we are caught in the middle of that struggle.

Two Paths to Follow

Before we look at the specifics of God's plan, let's look again at the underlying blueprint that sets the scene. The fact that we are faced with a choice between two paths lays the groundwork for our being transformed. Proverbs 3:5–6 says, "Trust in the LORD with all your heart; do not depend on your own understanding. Seek his will in all you do, and he will show you which path to take." I've usually heard this passage quoted as an encouragement to trust God more or as instruction for how we find God's will for our lives. But the phrase that grabs my attention is that God will show me "which path to take." Think of the battle we just described as being a turf war over two different paths that are open to us. Transformation begins by giving the right answer to the question of which path we are going to take.

If you did a study on the word *path* in the Bible, you would begin to see clearly the blueprint for God's plan for transforming our minds. Over and over, there are references to the two paths on which we can choose to live our lives. Sometimes a translation uses the word *way* or *road*, but the idea is the same: there are two ways we can live our lives. One is to travel on God's path and follow his design; the other is to travel on what we might call the "secular" path. The Bible describes this path with terms like *the flesh, the world,* and *our sinful nature,* as well as some other terms.

We noted earlier that Jeremiah described this choice between the two paths to the people of Jerusalem. He was warning them about the coming fall of that great city and about how its people would be captured and taken into exile by the Babylonians. He pointed out that Jerusalem and the kingdom of Judah would fall because the people were living life on the wrong path. When he promised that those who chose the right way, the ancient path, would find rest for their souls, one wonders who *wouldn't* want to walk on that path.

But the people answered Jeremiah by saying, "We will not walk in it" (Jer. 6:16 NIV).

Transformation begins as we ask for the ancient path, or as some translations say, "Ask for the old, godly way" (Jer. 6:16 NLT). From the beginning, God has prepared a path, a way for us to live, that is good and restful. But from the beginning, the other path—the path of the secular world, or of the flesh—is there beckoning us, and it is often just too enticing. We all live by our senses. And our senses are connected to the world around us. We experience a sight, a sound, a smell, a flavor, or a touch, and it feels good. It can easily set off our imagination in a wide variety of ways—some good, some evil. Then we can add to our senses our preprogrammed subconscious mind with its unconscious needs and desires, many of which come from unmet needs and desires as a child. You can see how easy it is to choose and to follow the world's path and to ignore the ancient path.

James describes what happens when we take the world's path. We are tempted, and "temptation comes from our own desires, which entice us and drag us away. These desires give birth to sinful actions. And when sin is allowed to grow, it gives birth to death" (James 1:14–15).

The Bible says what happens to those who stay on the world's path, or the path of the flesh. In Psalm 1:6, the writer says, "the path of the wicked leads to destruction." In Proverbs 2, we read, "Wisdom will save you from evil people, from those whose words are twisted. These men turn from the right way to walk down dark paths. They take pleasure in doing wrong, and they enjoy the twisted ways of evil. Their actions are crooked, and their ways are wrong" (vv. 12–15). Proverbs 4:14 warns us, "Don't do as the wicked do, and don't follow the path of evildoers." In Proverbs 7, men are warned to not even go near the house of an immoral woman, and the passage summarizes by saying, "Don't let your hearts stray away toward her. Don't wander down her wayward path" (v. 25).

Isaiah refers to "crooked roads, and no one who follows them knows a moment's peace" (Isa. 59:8). Jeremiah notes that those on this path are stubborn and hopeless. When he warns them of what is to come if they don't get off their evil path, they say to him, "Don't waste your breath. We will continue to live as we want to, stubbornly following our own evil desires" (Jer. 18:12). There is not even a hint of the desire for transformation for those in these passages who are on that path leading to destruction.

When we come to the New Testament, Jesus warns, "The highway to hell is broad, and its gate is wide for the many who choose that way" (Matt. 7:13). Paul has a rich vocabulary when he describes the way of what he calls the flesh, or our sinful nature. In writing to the Galatians, he says, "The sinful nature wants to do evil, which is just the opposite of what the Spirit wants. . . . These two forces are constantly fighting each other, so you are not free to carry out your good intentions" (Gal. 5:17). He then goes on to describe the intentions of the flesh, saying, "The results are very clear: sexual immorality, impurity, lustful pleasures, idolatry, sorcery, hostility, quarreling, jealousy, outbursts of anger, selfish ambition, dissension, division, envy, drunkenness, wild parties, and other sins like these" (Gal. 5:19–21). He starts with the more obvious evils, and then he gets down to things all of us struggle with, like envy or selfish ambition. You get the idea that he understands the war within us.

In Ephesians 4, Paul gives a more general description of those who walk on this path: "Their minds are full of darkness; they wander far from the life God gives because they have closed their minds and hardened their hearts against him. They have no sense of shame. They live for lustful pleasure and eagerly practice every kind of impurity" (vv. 18–19). In the next chapter, he mentions other temptations such as "obscene stories, foolish talk, and coarse jokes" (Eph. 5:4). All of these things are the result of walking on the world's well-worn path that leads to stress, misery, and eventually destruction. God never meant for us to experience life like that.

Peter adds his voice when he tells those who want to walk God's path to "get rid of all evil behavior. Be done with all deceit, hypocrisy, jealousy, and all unkind speech" (1 Peter 2:1). That's the world's path, and it leads to despair. We are all too often left with the hopelessness that Paul describes when he exclaims, "Oh, what a miserable person I am! Who will free me from this life that is dominated by sin and death?" (Rom. 7:24).

The Bible also describes the ancient path, the way toward peace. The Psalms are full of examples of the ancient path and its rewards. The psalmist writes that God "will show me the way of life, granting me the joy of your presence and the pleasures of living with you forever" (Ps. 16:11). David says, "My steps have stayed on your path; I have not wavered from following you" (Ps. 17:5). He also writes, "Show me the right path, O LORD; point out the road for me to follow. Lead me by your truth and teach me, for you are the God who saves me. All day long I put my hope in you" (Ps. 25:4–5).

Proverbs tells us, "Follow the steps of good men instead, and stay on the paths of the righteous" (2:20). Wisdom will "guide you down delightful paths; all her ways are satisfying" (3:17). A good father, speaking to his son, says, "I will teach you wisdom's ways and lead you in straight paths" (4:11). In addition, we are called to "walk in righteousness, in paths of justice" (8:20). Isaiah tells us the day will come when "many nations will come and say, 'Come, let us go up to the mountain of the LORD, to the house of Jacob's God. There he will teach us his ways, and we will walk in his paths'" (Isa. 2:3).

Did you notice the pleasurable things we can experience on this ancient path? The world's path always entices us, telling us what we will miss if we get on the ancient path. But God answers the world with promises of hope, delight, straight paths, and justice, and that's just the beginning. Paul describes the ancient path as our walking in the Spirit, and the results are "love, joy, peace, patience, kindness, goodness, faithfulness, gentleness, and self-control" (Gal. 5:22–23). And then Paul says that when we are on God's path, we will "experience God's peace, which exceeds anything we can understand" (Phil. 4:7). This is what we will enjoy when we live by the Spirit of God. If we really want transformation, it begins when we choose to walk on the ancient path.

The Battle Is On

What do we fight when we struggle against our inner programming? Paul tells us that the battle is not what we imagine. He said, "We are human, but we don't wage war as humans do. We use God's mighty weapons, not worldly weapons, to knock down the strongholds of human reasoning and to destroy false arguments" (2 Cor. 10:3–4). The battleground is in the very place we are trying to renew—our mind. Remember, Paul was a Jew, and the Jewish meaning of the word *mind* includes our heart and can be summed up in the phrase "the center of our being." At the center of who we are—in our subconscious mind—there are strongholds of human reasoning and arguments that are against God. A stronghold is like a fortress, and inside these fortresses are proud arguments of human reasoning that the enemy of our soul will use to keep us off the ancient path.

But Paul doesn't leave us there. He gives us a practical example of God's plan for transformation. In that same passage he continues on to give us our strategy: "We destroy every proud obstacle that keeps people from knowing God. We capture their rebellious thoughts and teach them to obey Christ" (2 Cor. 10:5). We destroy these strongholds of human reasoning and arguments that are against God by taking captive every thought that comes into our mind and teaching each thought to obey Christ. We bring our thoughts—our belief systems—into obedience to what Christ wants and says. Paul is describing a process that leads to transformation.

God's Plan for Transformation

The ancient path that God calls us to walk is described all through Psalm 119. In verse 9, the psalmist begins with the question, "How can a young person stay pure?" and then answers it: "By obeying your word." In verse 11, the answer is expanded when the writer says, "I have hidden your word in my heart, that I might not sin against you."

How do we hide God's Word in our heart? What does the psalmist mean? Are we to memorize Scripture? Is that it? That certainly is part of what the psalmist means. But let's look at what the Bible says about hiding God's Word in our heart.

To better understand what the psalmist means by hiding God's Word in our heart, we can look at two events in Mary's life. The Bible says that the shepherds were told by the angel to go and find the baby Jesus, and "after seeing him, the shepherds told everyone what had happened and what the angel had said to them about this child. All who heard the shepherds' story were astonished, but Mary kept all these things in her heart and thought about them often" (Luke 2:17–19).

Twelve years later, when Jesus stayed back in Jerusalem after the Passover celebration, Joseph and Mary thought they had lost him. It took them three days to find him. When they did, they were amazed at what Jesus was doing. He was sitting in the temple with the religious leaders, interacting with these men who were "amazed at his understanding and his answers" (2:47). Later, when they returned with Jesus to Nazareth, it says that Mary "stored all these things in her heart" (2:51).

From the description of Mary's experience, we can say that hiding God's Word in our heart means we store, or keep, God's words in our heart and mind, which involves both meditating on and memorizing Scripture. When we hide God's Word in our heart, we are also to ponder and think about those words often throughout the day. That's what is called meditating on his Word. What Mary did was what brain scientists suggest we do if we are to change the pathways in our brain—we are to focus our attention on something. For any who choose the ancient way, our focus of attention is on God's Word. It means we commit Scripture to memory or meditate on it, and then we are to think on it often. Focused attention is called, even by the brain scientists, *meditation*.

Now when we use that word *meditation*, some people are rightly concerned. There are legitimate fears about some forms of meditation. Usually those fears are tied to Eastern thought and the type of meditation found in Eastern religions. There, the goal of meditation is to empty the mind of everything. The focus is on some mantra with the intention of coming to a place where the mind is empty.

But Jesus warns against this. When the religious teachers and the Pharisees were saying to themselves that Jesus's power came from Satan, Jesus tells them he is casting out demons by the power of God. Then he says, "When an evil spirit leaves a person, it goes into the desert, searching for rest. But when it finds none, it says, 'I will return to the person I came from.' So it returns and finds that its former home is all swept and in order. Then the spirit finds seven other spirits more

evil than itself, and they all enter the person and live there"
(Luke 11:24–26). The house had been emptied—nothing
was there. Jesus is implying that when we clear our mind so
that nothing remains, we are leaving an opening for the old
patterns to not only return but also to bring their evil friends
with them.

Meditation is not the exclusive domain of Eastern reli-
gions—it is to be a part of the life of every disciple of Jesus.
To better understand what Psalm 119 says about how we hide
God's Word in our heart, we need to note that in the style of
Hebrew poetry, the writer uses ten different words that all
refer to God's Word. Whenever we encounter one of these
other words, I will remind you that it refers to God's Word.
The psalmist writes these things about meditation:

> Joyful are those who obey his laws [Word]
> and search for him with all their hearts. (v. 2)

> I will study your commandments [Word]
> and reflect on your ways [Word]. (v. 15)

> I will meditate on your decrees [Word]. (v. 23)

> I will meditate on your wonderful deeds
> [Word]. . . .
> Encourage me by your word. (vv. 27–28)

> How I delight in your commands [Word]!
> How I love them! (v. 47)

> I meditate on your age-old regulations [Word];
> O LORD, they comfort me. (v. 52)

I will concentrate on your commandments
　　[Word]. (v. 78)

Though the wicked hide along the way to kill me,
　　I will quietly keep my mind on your laws
　　[Word]. (v. 95)

Oh, how I love your instructions [Word]!
　　I think about them all day long. (v. 97)

Your word is a lamp to guide my feet
　　and a light for my path. (v. 105)

I stay awake through the night,
　　thinking about your promise [Word]. (v. 148)

I rejoice in your word
　　like one who discovers a great treasure. (v. 162)

All of Psalm 119 is rich in guidelines for those who seek transformation, and it all centers on hiding God's words within the center of our being through meditation, then pondering and thinking on those words throughout the day and the night. This type of meditation is called *discursive meditation*, for it has a focus: it is focused on Scripture. The purpose of Christian meditation is to focus our attention in such a way that it changes our lives at even the level of our subconscious mind!

But you say, "I've been reading the Bible for years, and I still haven't experienced the transformation that is promised in the Bible." Perhaps this illustration will show the difference in reading the Bible as opposed to in-depth meditation on the Bible. Often the way we read the Bible isn't much different from how we read the sports page or the business section of the newspaper. We read for information, for knowledge. There is nothing wrong with this type of reading, but this alone will not lead to transformation. It is focused on facts and data, not on transformation.

In contrast, imagine a couple who is deeply in love, but for a period of time they are separated from each other by great distance. During this separation, they exchange letters that are deep expressions of their love and devotion for each other. Now imagine that one of them gets one of these deeply personal letters filled with loving thoughts. How do they read the letter? Do they read it like the sports page and then put it aside? Of course not. They read it slowly, and then they reread every word, pondering every thought expressed in the letter. They read it so often they end up memorizing parts of the letter that are particularly poignant and meaningful. They have moved from a simple reading to a discursive meditation on the letter. They may spend an hour reading and savoring everything on the page (or the computer), allowing the words to become a part of themselves. That's what the Bible means when it speaks of meditation. That's what is called discursive meditation.

Eugene Peterson, in his book titled *Eat This Book*, refers to the passage in Revelation 10 that tells of a mighty angel who has one foot on the land and the other on the sea, and he begins preaching from a small scroll, which is the Bible. John, the writer of Revelation, says he is about to write what the angel is saying. But a voice from heaven says, "Do not write it down" (v. 4). So John puts down his pen, and then he is told to go up to the angel and ask for the scroll—the Bible. As he does, the angel says to him, "'Yes, take it and eat it. . . . It will be sweet as honey in your mouth, but it will turn sour in your stomach!' So I took the small scroll from the hand of the angel, and I ate it! It was sweet in my mouth, but when I swallowed it, it turned sour in my stomach" (vv. 9–10).[1]

What an interesting image this presents to us. He is told to "eat" the book. But it wasn't the first time someone in the Bible was told to "eat" that book. The prophet Jeremiah said, "When I discovered your words, I devoured them. They are my joy and my heart's delight" (Jer. 15:16). During his call by God, Ezekiel was told,

> "Open your mouth, and eat what I give you." Then I looked and saw a hand reaching out to me. It held a scroll, which he unrolled. And I saw that both sides were covered with funeral songs, words of sorrow, and pronouncements of doom. The voice said to me, "Son of man, eat what I am giving you—eat this scroll! Then go and give its message to the people of Israel." (Ezek. 2:8–3:1)

Both prophets were told to eat the scroll and then go deliver the message.

How does a person "eat" the Bible? Obviously, we don't literally eat it, but we can figuratively. Some years ago, my wife and I spent several days together at a monastery to do a silent retreat. Before we started the three-day period of silence, we talked with one of the monks about what we should do with our time. He suggested we follow a centuries-old method of reading the Bible, and he went on to describe it to us using an analogy of eating. Here's what he suggested and what we did—and still do.

First, he said we were to think of reading the Bible as if we were perusing a menu. For example, he told us to take a short passage, such as a paragraph in the part of the Bible we were each choosing to read, and read it over three or four times slowly and prayerfully. This is an attitude of respect that honors the Scripture. He suggested we might even want to read it out loud. He told us to let the text speak to us. Just as when we read over a menu, something grabs our attention, and that's what we order, he encouraged us to read a passage over and over until a phrase or a word grabbed our attention, and then we were to continue on to phase two of spiritual reading.

The second phase is similar to what happens when the food has been served and you begin to eat your meal. You take a bite and slowly begin to chew it. As you do, you savor the taste of what you are eating, noticing the spices and the nuances of the flavors. It's much like what John said in Revelation 10, when he took a bite of the book and found that it was "sweet as honey" in his mouth. You focus your attention on the flavors of the phrase or word that you have chosen. You "chew it over" in your mind, thinking of what it means to you and what it says to you. You let the word or phrase speak to you in your heart.

For example, as I was writing this, my wife just brought me a sliced white peach. I could have gulped it down and eaten my fruit for the day. But instead, I slowly took each piece and savored the sweetness and the freshness of a wonderful, ripe white peach. I chewed it slowly, letting the flavors linger in my mouth. Even after I had swallowed a piece, the flavor lasted. That's what I want to do when I have found that phrase or word in a passage that has grabbed my attention. I want to savor it!

After some time chewing, you swallow what you are eating. In your spiritual reading, this means you prayerfully begin to personalize what you have been chewing on. At this point, you ponder the thoughts that have flowed into your mind based on the phrase or word. You prayerfully open yourself to what God is saying to you. You are letting the Holy Spirit bring the meaning of this passage deep within your soul—down where it penetrates even your subconscious mind.

When we eat, digestion automatically follows. We don't consciously think about digesting our food, but as digestion takes place, nutrients are sent to the appropriate parts of our body to strengthen us. In the same way, as we quietly contemplate what God has been saying to us, we digest it and allow it to touch some area of our life that needs to be confronted, some area where we are struggling, or some area where we need to be strengthened or comforted. We digest the words and then go about our day continuing to think on what we have digested. It's like what Mary did—we think about what God has said to us often throughout the day and even return to those thoughts as they come to us. We ponder them in our hearts.

When John the apostle swallowed the book, he said it turned sour in his stomach. That would be like me meditating on a passage of Scripture and, as I contemplate its meaning and its application to my life, being challenged or confronted by what the passage says. At first the passage tastes sweet, but as I ponder it, it convicts me of sin or challenges me in some area where I need to grow.

That's what happened to Jack when he received the hurtful email from his sister. Earlier he had meditated on the passage in Ephesians, memorizing those two verses, and then had thought about them at various times over the following days. The part of those two verses that had penetrated deep within him was "be kind to each other, tenderhearted." He had been convicted of a need to grow in his attitude toward others. Because he had spent time meditating on that phrase, it had become a part of him, and the Holy Spirit could easily bring it to his mind when it was needed. Jack knew the experience of "swallowing" the book and finding that it was sour in his stomach, for he had been confronted about an important part of his life that needed transformation.

This is a different kind of reading than what we often do. Eugene Peterson says, "We do not read this book . . . in order to get God into our lives, to get him to participate in our lives. No. We open this book and find that page after page it takes us off guard, surprises us, and draws us into its reality, pulls us into participation with God on His terms."[2]

In this kind of immersion in the Bible, we don't read the text to get advice or support, nor do we read to be able to say to ourselves we've had our "quiet time." Instead, we read slowly and meditatively, without expectation except for the hope that in our reading we will have an encounter with the living God.

That's what happened to St. Augustine when he read the Bible prayerfully and meditatively. God's Word spoke directly to him, and his life was changed radically. He experienced transformation. James Finley says, "If you are going to be a fair-weather meditator, meditating only occasionally in moments that seem conducive to it, you are likely to avoid many of the challenges a commitment to daily meditation can bring. But then again you will also miss out on the full potential of self-transformation and spiritual fulfillment that meditation provides."[3]

The Spirit of God works through the Word of God as we prayerfully approach it in a disciplined way. This is God's plan for transformation.

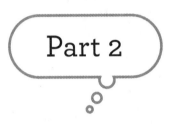

Part 2

Now that we have looked at the basics of how our brains work, we turn to the specifics of how we can experience God's transforming power in our lives. We hide God's words in our hearts through meditation and memorization. And then we ponder God's words throughout our day. So let's begin our journey of renewing our minds through meditation by looking at some of the things many of us want to change.

In each of the next chapters, we will look at a specific issue we may struggle with in our lives. We will begin each chapter by identifying the problem, then we will consider what goes on in our brain related to that specific issue. Our focus will then shift to meditating on Scriptures that relate to what God wants us to understand about that problem. Then we will consider another group of Scriptures that will help us understand more clearly God's desired solution.

The Scripture passages are grouped together, making it easy for you to "eat" the passage. As you meditate on the Scriptures, note things that stand out to you. You may find it helpful to journal about what God says to you in each passage. Following your meditation on the passage and your reflections on what struck you, come back throughout the day to what the passage said to you. Again, think about what you read—ponder it. And especially think of it again as you end your day. Remember, God's Word is alive and seeks to be active in our lives. Not every chapter may speak to a current struggle in your life. So feel free to focus on the chapters that are relevant to your needs.

5

Moving from Fear to Love

We saw in an earlier chapter that the amygdala in our brain operates primarily on fear, so let's begin the process of renewing the center of our being by desensitizing the fear response of our amygdala. Why is fear paired with love in the title of this chapter? Because the apostle John wisely points out that the opposite of fear is love: "Such love has no fear, because perfect love expels all fear. If we are afraid, it is for fear of punishment, and this shows that we have not fully experienced his perfect love" (1 John 4:18). John is saying that when love is perfect, fear is absent, banished. But since only God can love perfectly, and we love imperfectly, our ability to love will always be tainted to some degree by our fears.

Think of it this way. When I am in love with a person or with something, I want to move toward the one I love. When a teenager "falls in love," they want to be with the person they think they love. They text, talk, meet at the mall—anything to create the opportunity to be together.

Or think of a person who loves chocolate. When they go to the mall, they park in a certain place so that when they go inside, they walk right by the store that sells chocolate and they can purchase what they love. And of course, when they leave the mall, they pass right by the same store and will buy some more so they can "be together" at home. Love is always movement *toward*.

When I ask an audience to tell me what they think is the opposite of love, I usually get either "anger" or "indifference" as the answer. Experientially, these may seem like they are the opposites of love, and indifference may come close. But anger really is not the opposite of love, for the movement of anger is similar to the movement of love. The movement of anger, as we will see more in the next chapter, is movement *against*. It is movement in the same direction as love, but with intensity. It is the "fight" part in the amygdala's fight-or-flight response to a threat against us. And the movement either pushes someone away or strikes out against the object of the threat. But it moves in the same direction as love—toward.

The movement of fear is *away from*. It is the flight part of our fight-or-flight response. When I am fearful, I want to run, or, depending on the nature of the threat, I may freeze. When I freeze, it is because my appraisal of the threat is that it is too overpowering and I can't run fast enough to get away—so I freeze instead.

I talked with a young man recently who was very isolated. Samuel defined himself as a "loner." What bothered him was that he was attracted to a certain young woman at church. But when he thought of talking to her, the terror he felt paralyzed him. He longed to be able to talk with her, but he couldn't. He couldn't even talk to his one friend about his struggle. He was simply too afraid. So he took a big risk and decided to come to a counselor for help.

As we talked together, it was clear that he had some strong feelings about this young woman and they were totally appropriate. But his fear was stronger than his feelings of love and attraction. Until he could get to the root of his fears, his ability to express his loving feelings for this woman was totally blocked by that fear.

Why Are We So Dominated by Fear?

Why was Samuel so paralyzed? There could be several reasons. For one, fear is part of the consequence of both our own sins and the sins that were done to us. In Genesis 2:25, which precedes the introduction of sin into humanity, Adam and Eve "were both naked, but they felt no shame." Shame is a part of the fear response, so their feeling no shame includes the idea that they were not afraid of their love and intimacy.

Then in Genesis 3:10 we get the rest of the story. After Adam and Eve disobeyed God, they hid from him. When God asked where they were, Adam responded by saying, "I hid. I was afraid because I was naked." So one of the consequences of sin is that we have this struggle with fear.

Another reason we struggle with fear was described in chapter 2. Our amygdala is our brain's warning system that a threat or danger is nearby. When our ancestors were moving west across the United States in wagon trains, the fear orientation of their amygdala was very important. Threats from hostile Indians, rugged terrain, or physical illnesses had to be monitored. Their amygdala was on duty at all times, seeking to protect them.

As the warning system, our amygdala is basically oriented in the direction of fear. Long ago it meant survival; today it means that we struggle with fears, worries, anxiety, and shame almost to a fault. In many cases, there is no basis in reality for our fears—they're simply the fundamental orientation of our amygdala.

But more specifically, the strength of our struggle with the emotion of fear has a lot to do with those early developmental years—between birth and age six or seven. One of the things that happens during those years is that we have mirroring neurons that are learning new behaviors. A simple illustration is the behavior of my one-year-old granddaughter. I was with her recently and we were playing. I looked surprised and covered my eyes, and then watched as she looked surprised and covered her eyes. I got down on my knees and she did the same. Over and over she mirrored exactly what I did. Her mirroring neurons were active.

So let's imagine that for some reason Samuel's mom was fearful and very uncomfortable around strangers. As a stranger approached little Samuel and his mother, he saw a look of fear come over her face. Samuel mirrored the look on the mother's face, and this laid the groundwork of a basic fear of strangers. Other experiences during those early years add to and expand his fear response. Years later, a grown-up Samuel is controlled not only by a fear of strangers but by a fear of any new relationship. And he has no awareness of where that fear was first generated.

How Meditation Overcomes Fear

So how do we reprogram the amygdala to be less fearful? How do we overcome a fear-based lifestyle and move to a love-based lifestyle? Here's what I did with Samuel. I began talking to him about the power of God's Word to change our lives, that somehow we needed to "eat" the Word. I went over the principles described in the previous chapter and then suggested he begin by meditating on passages where God directly challenges our fears. I also asked him to simply meditate on the words "Fear not." Every time an angel appeared to anyone in the Bible, his first words were "Fear not" or "Don't be afraid." This is where Samuel started his healing process. Then I pointed him to other passages in Scripture that I wanted him to focus on. Below are the passages I suggested to him. If you struggle with being fearful, I suggest that you spend time meditating on them as well.

> The LORD is my light and my salvation—
>   so why should I be afraid?
> The LORD is my fortress, protecting me from danger,
>   so why should I tremble?

When evil people come to devour me,
    when my enemies and foes attack me,
    they will stumble and fall.
Though a mighty army surrounds me,
    my heart will not be afraid.
Even if I am attacked,
    I will remain confident.[1]

He will cover you with his feathers.
    He will shelter you with his wings.
    His faithful promises are your armor and
        protection.
Do not be afraid of the terrors of the night,
    nor the arrow that flies in the day.
Do not dread the disease that stalks in darkness,
    nor the disaster that strikes at midday.[2]

They do not fear bad news;
    they confidently trust the Lord to care for
        them.[3]

Say to those with fearful hearts,
    "Be strong, and do not fear,
for your God is coming to destroy your enemies.
    He is coming to save you."[4]

Don't be afraid, for I am with you.
    Don't be discouraged, for I am your God.
I will strengthen you and help you.
    I will hold you up with my victorious right hand.[5]

Fear not; you will no longer live in shame.
    Don't be afraid; there is no more disgrace for
        you.[6]

Who would not fear you, O King of nations?
>   That title belongs to you alone! . . .
>   There is no one like you.[7]

Yes, you came when I called;
>   you told me, "Do not fear."[8]

Son of man, do not fear them or their words. Don't be afraid even though their threats surround you. . . . Do not be dismayed by their dark scowls.[9]

So you have not received a spirit that makes you fearful slaves. Instead, you received God's Spirit when he adopted you as his own children. Now we call him, "Abba Father."[10]

And I am convinced that nothing can ever separate us from God's love. Neither death nor life, neither angels nor demons, neither our fears for today nor our worries about tomorrow—not even the powers of hell can separate us from God's love.[11]

For God has not given us a spirit of fear and timidity, but of power, love, and self-discipline.[12]

Such love has no fear; because perfect love expels all fear. If we are afraid, it is for fear of punishment, and this shows that we have not fully experienced his perfect love.[13]

As I did with Samuel, I suggest you spend twenty to thirty minutes a day at least four times a week focusing on these verses. Read a passage slowly three to four times, allowing its message to sink into your heart and mind. You may want to look up the reference to a particular verse in order to put it in context, and then read several of the verses that surround the passage. As God's truth sinks in, help it go deeper by making it your prayer. Pray it into your soul. Then just sit quietly as you digest its truth. Finally, pause throughout the day and think about what the passage says.

The Two Paths Associated with Fear

When it comes to fear, the world's path tells us to simply hide our fears. Wear a T-shirt that says "No Fear" and act that way. Hollywood's answer to a fear-based life is to push us to become aggressive about life, especially in the sexual arena. Sexual conquests will cure your fears, Hollywood tells us.

But God's path—the ancient path—tells us that when we focus on our relationship with God and how much he loves us, we will grow beyond our fears. We will live more in the reality of the law of love. That's why the apostle John says that the more we experience God's perfect way of loving us, the more we cast out fear from our lives. And we become increasingly free to love. Again, there are two paths and the choice is ours.

What Is This Thing Called Love?

The song says that "love is a many-splendored thing," and it certainly is multidimensional. The Greeks had four words to describe love. To them, and to the early Christian community, the highest form of love was called *agape.* It was considered an unconditional, sacrificial form of love. It was used to describe the way God loves us unconditionally. Second, the Greeks used the word *philia*, which referred to a brotherly kind of love. The word is the root of the name Philadelphia, which is called "the city of brotherly love." Third, they referred to *storge*, which is an affectionate type of love we might have for our family members. And fourth, they describe *eros* as a passionate, sensual, and romantic love that could be depicted by Cupid with his arrows.

Researcher Robert Sternberg gives an interesting description of love in his book *The Triangle of Love.*[14] He defines love as having three facets: intimacy, passion, and commitment. Out of these three facets, we can describe seven different types of love. If we have intimacy alone, our love is really "liking" someone, what the Greeks would call platonic love or *philia* love. If we have passion alone, we have romantic love—or we might call it infatuation. If we have commitment alone, we have an empty form of love. I have a neighbor who was married for over sixty years, and when his wife died, he was very open about describing his hatred of her. But they were committed!

What if we have only intimacy and passion? This is what I call the Hollywood form of love. It's the type of love we see in the movies or read about in romance novels. There is a physical attraction that draws the two people together, they sleep together, but there is no commitment to keep them together. Sometimes they marry, but they don't stay together very long.

If we have intimacy and commitment, we have a "good enough" form of love. But there is no passion.

And when we have passion and commitment, we might say it's the form of love that fills the pages of *People* magazine. There is a passion that draws two people together and a commitment that holds them together for a time, but there is no sense of wanting to know the other person. The commitment is based on passion, which doesn't last much more than a year or so.

Real love requires all three components: intimacy, passion, and commitment. We can see this as the foundation of a fulfilling marriage. Both the husband and the wife grow in knowing their spouse. Their passion is sexual, but it is more than that. They enjoy being together. And they are committed to each other. Couples who stay together have found a way to incorporate all three facets into their relationship. We can also see this in our love relationships with our children. We know them at a deep level. We enjoy them and take pleasure in what they do and say—that's a fuller definition of passion. And we are committed to them, at least until they grow up and go their own way.

What Happens in Our Brain When We Love

All forms of love live in our brain, and many of the same parts of the brain that are involved in sexual and romantic love can be activated as well by drugs, by music, and even by intense spiritual and religious activity. The major part of the brain that is involved in love resides in the limbic system.

The amygdala plays a key role in determining whether an experience is pleasurable or not, and whether it should be repeated or avoided.

Just as in the fear response, when we experience any form of love, the amygdala sends a message to the hypothalamus to release different hormones into our system than when we are stressed or afraid. The amygdala then tells the hippocampus to record memories of the event. We can understand this if we first look at what happens in the early stages of love, or what might be called the stage of infatuation.

When we first fall in love, we are literally in an altered state of consciousness. The limbic system is flooded with a special cocktail of hormones and neurotransmitters. Dopamine is increased, as is norepinephrine. A neurotransmitter called phenylethylamine, or PEA, is also released. When we are under the influence of this powerful cocktail, we have an amazingly positive attitude about everything. We will experience increased energy, a decreased need for sleep, and a loss of appetite. We call it "feeling the chemistry" for a reason—it's based on brain chemistry!

We make light of this stage of love, even calling it "puppy love," but there are some very important lessons we can learn from someone caught up in the chemistry of this early stage of love. Here are some of the behaviors we see in the infatuation stage that can be applied to any loving relationship, even to our relationship with God:

We make the relationship a priority.
We make each other's needs a priority.

We are positive about our future.

We laugh and play—we enjoy each other.

We accept our differences.

Unfortunately—or maybe it is fortunate—the chemical cocktail in our brain begins to wind down after about twelve months, and then in the second year of the relationship, it is gone. It has served its purpose—it has brought two people together. Now the work of loving begins, and the brain co-operates by creating a different cocktail—a comfort cocktail.

Look at this spiritually in terms of our relationship with God. When we first give our lives to Christ, we are excited. We can't get enough of the Word of God or preaching or worship. We are in love with Jesus! And rightly so. That level of loving God is also easy in the early stages, for the same chemical cocktail is at work in our brain. God put it there to get us started in our discipleship with him. But that level of loving, even loving God, doesn't last automatically. We have to make it last, and that's where meditation and community with other believers takes over.

In the same way, in our earthly relationships and marriage, we need the chemistry of infatuation, or of falling in love, to overcome our fear of intimacy and to bring us together. But when the cocktail wears off, the real work of love must begin. Unfortunately there are too many people who fall in love with falling in love, and they try to re-create the chemistry in their brain that they experienced at the beginning of loving.

We see the same thing in those who start strong in their relationship with the Lord, only to falter after a couple of years. They are like the seed in Jesus's parable that falls on the rocky soil. It sprouts, but its roots don't go deep, and when the heat of summer comes, it withers and dies (see Luke 8:4–15). Perhaps that's why Webster defines *infatuation* as "shallow love."

But there is something that takes place in the brain that sets in motion the next stage of love, which is the place where true love begins. Now the pleasure center of the brain becomes more active. This part of the brain is also in the limbic system. Remember that everything that goes on in the limbic system is unconscious. We don't have direct control of it, although we can activate it through our behaviors.

What is called the pleasure center of our brain, or the reward center, involves the *nucleus accumbens*, which is just behind the frontal cortex in the ventral segmental area, or VTS. This part of the brain is embedded close to the center of the limbic system. As the infatuation chemistry is fading away, the positive behaviors have activated the pleasure center. The experience is sent down the VTS pathway of the brain for evaluation, which then sends its rating to the amygdala and the prefrontal cortex—the executive part of our brain, where we are conscious of what has just occurred.

What is happening is that the infatuation cocktail is being replaced by a more comfortable cocktail. Over time, true love involves the blending and balance of more than one hundred different hormones and neurochemical transmitter substances. For example, lust is driven by testosterone in both males and females. Norepinephrine and dopamine are also involved. It's interesting that when a man holds a baby in his arms, his testosterone levels go down. One might say he is being domesticated.

This comfort cocktail, though, has at its center the hormone oxytocin, which is sometimes called the "cuddle hormone." It is the hormone that drives our ability to attach and to bond with another person. It's what a mother experiences when she holds her baby. It's what a couple experiences when they achieve orgasm. It's what a wife experiences when her husband holds her hand in a threatening situation.

The cocktail of true love is also made up of the hormone vasopressin. Vasopressin primarily regulates the body's retention of water, but it also acts much like oxytocin in that it facilitates the circuits in the brain responsible for bonding.

To go back to our triangle of love—intimacy, passion, and commitment—the infatuation cocktail facilitates the passion and desire for intimacy, for knowing the other person, at the beginning of the relationship. But then oxytocin and vasopressin facilitate the commitment stage of true love. They also offset what can be the crazy passion of lust driven by testosterone, dopamine, and norepinephrine.

Moving from Fear to Love

C. S. Lewis described love this way: "Love, in the Christian sense, does not mean an emotion. It is a state not of the feelings but of the will; that state of the will which we have naturally about ourselves and must learn to have about other people."[15] What does he mean by "in the Christian sense"? Basically he is saying that what Jesus taught us about love is different from what our culture tells us about love.

For example, in John's Gospel, Jesus tells the disciples, "This is my commandment: Love each other in the same way I have loved you" (15:12). How can you command someone to love if it is only an emotion? Can someone just conjure up the emotion of love, or is love more than an emotion, as Lewis is saying? Earlier in the same chapter, Jesus couples loving with obeying. He says, "When you obey my commandments, you remain in my love, just as I obey my Father's commandments and remain in his love" (v. 10).

And what about the great love chapter? Have you ever noticed there isn't a single emotion described in 1 Corinthians 13? The apostle Paul defines love totally in behavioral terms: "Love is patient and kind. Love is not jealous or boastful or proud or rude. It does not demand its own way. It is not irritable, and it keeps no record of being wronged. It does not rejoice about injustice but rejoices whenever the truth wins out. Love never gives up, never loses faith, is always hopeful, and endures through every circumstance" (vv. 4–7). This is what love is when we are on God's path. Let's look at the differences in the world's path and his.

> The world says, "You fall in love and you fall out of love."
> God says, "Love is based on a commitment and the behaviors of love."
> The world says, "Once you stop loving, it's over."

God says, "Love never fails."

The world says, "I still love you, but I'm not *in love* with you anymore."

God says, "The LORD witnessed the vows you and your wife made when you were young. But you have been unfaithful to her" (Mal. 2:14).

The world says, "Get even."

God says, "Love your enemies."

We could go on and highlight the differences between what we are told love is and what God considers love to be. Since God defines love through behaviors, we have a choice. We can show love through our behaviors, or we can buy into our culture's lies about the true nature of love. And the interesting thing that happens when we choose God's path is that the emotions we associate with love begin to grow stronger and stronger.

If you've been meditating on the "fearless" passages, you should experience a reduction in your fear levels. But it is not enough to just take something away; more importantly, we must replace what has been taken away with its opposite. So now take some time to meditate on the following passages that encourage us to love. Again, spend twenty to thirty minutes a day at least four days a week focusing on each passage. Add the verses that provide the context as you meditate on the passage.

> Your love for one another will prove to the world that you are my disciples.[16]

I have loved you even as the Father has loved me. Remain in my love.[17]

There is no greater love than to lay down one's life for one's friends. You are my friends if you do what I command.[18]

Love each other with genuine affection, and take delight in honoring each other.[19]

Owe nothing to anyone—except for your obligation to love one another. If you love your neighbor, you will fulfill the requirements of God's law.[20]

Love does no wrong to others, so love fulfills the requirements of God's law.[21]

For you have been called to live in freedom, my brothers and sisters. But don't use your freedom to satisfy your sinful nature. Instead, use your freedom to serve one another in love.[22]

Get rid of all bitterness, rage, anger, harsh words, and slander, as well as all types of evil behavior. Instead, be kind to each other, tenderhearted, forgiving one another, just as God through Christ has forgiven you.[23]

May the Lord make your love for one another and for all people grow and overflow, just as our love for you overflows.[24]

But we don't need to write to you about the importance of loving each other, for God himself has taught you to love one another.[25]

Let us think of ways to motivate one another to acts of love and good works.[26]

Dear friends, I am not writing a new commandment for you; rather it is an old one you have had from the very beginning. This old commandment—to love one another—is the same message you heard before.[27]

And this is his commandment: We must believe in the name of his Son, Jesus Christ, and love one another, just as he commanded us.[28]

Dear friends, let us continue to love one another, for love comes from God. Anyone who loves is a child of God and knows God.[29]

Love means doing what God has commanded us, and he has commanded us to love one another, just as you heard from the beginning.[30]

One cannot overstate the importance of loving one another as an outgrowth of our relationship with God through Jesus Christ. It's central to what Jesus taught the disciples. You may want to spend some time meditating on what is called the "upper room discourse," John 13–16, where Jesus spends very personal time with the disciples to help them overcome their fears. When you read Paul's epistles, you will notice how often he replaces the old law, with its rules and regulations, with what could be called the law of love. In the Romans 13 passages above, Paul says that love fulfills the requirements of God's law! What a promise we have as we learn to love and, in so doing, cast out all fear.

6

Moving from Anger to Forgiveness

Tyler was brilliant. He'd always been brilliant. It had not been a surprise to anyone attending his tenth high school reunion that he had risen to the position he held in his investment bank job. When he finished college, his firm had recruited him with the promise they would pay for his MBA, which he'd completed five years ago. He'd moved up quickly in the firm's hierarchy, and so had his income. He already had close to six figures in his personal investments, and he had just turned thirty.

He was the rising star at the bank, clearly on a path to the top. It seemed like nothing could stop him. Nothing, that is, until he was passed over for a promotion that everyone thought was a lock for him. It threw him off balance. When he heard he had not gotten the promotion, he quickly met with his immediate boss. He was hurt and he was angry. But he kept it under control, for he was desperate to know what had gone wrong. He practically begged his boss to tell him what had happened.

At first his boss was reluctant to talk about it, but Tyler wouldn't let up. Finally, what came out was that the top brass of the bank, though pleased with Tyler's work, had started to worry about him. They felt there was an edge to him that would eventually work against him. Of course, their real worry was that it could eventually work against the success of the bank.

As Tyler drove home, it was only the other people's good driving skills that kept him from killing someone on the road. He was in a rage like he couldn't remember. When he got home, he put his fist through a wall, and then he threw a lamp against another wall, shattering it and putting a hole in that wall. His wife was terrified. Down deep, she had feared he was a walking time bomb with his anger, but up until today he had kept it in check. She asked carefully what had happened, but he didn't answer. He just grabbed his keys again and left.

He needed to work out his frustration, and speed had always helped. But when he was stopped for speeding, he just sat there in his car for the longest time, staring at the ticket. Then he broke down in sobs. Fortunately, no one was around, so he just sat there in his car and wept. As he gradually settled down, he headed back home again. As he walked toward his home office, he simply said to his wife, "I didn't get the job. I just want to be alone for now."

As he sat there, he knew he had an issue with his anger. He thought he had used the energy of that anger to sharpen his focus. But somehow the anger had leaked out without his even knowing it. Up to this point, that inner rage fueled his passion to work harder than anyone else. *How did it show?* he asked himself over and over.

Then he thought about his dad. Every day as he was growing up, his father would wake him up with a barrage of criticism like a Marine drill sergeant. As a kid, he couldn't argue back, so he just listened and quietly got ready for school. He knew he had been a disappointment to his father. His grades and his academic achievements had meant nothing to his dad. His father loved sports, and his dream was that his only son would love sports as well. He had always hoped he would see his son play on one of the high school teams. But Tyler had never been interested in playing a sport. Besides, he probably wasn't good enough to play on any high school team, except the debate team. There he had excelled!

Tyler's father died when Tyler was nineteen. It was during his first year at college, and he remembers that his father's death didn't mean that much to him. He didn't grieve for him. He tried to look sad at the funeral, but the service only seemed to remind him that his father had never really accepted him. If Tyler had felt any anger at his father, it was expressed more in his mind as "I'll show him." He had used his anger at his dad to provide the energy to excel in his job, but now that anger had failed him.

It seemed that every morning when Tyler woke up, he could still hear his dad's voice in his head, criticizing him. *Maybe Dad was right*, he thought. *Maybe I've just been fooling myself. Maybe I did turn out to be a nothing.* To Tyler, not getting the promotion was a failure, and he didn't know what to do with the image of himself as a failure. He'd never failed before.

Later that evening, as he talked with his wife, he realized she couldn't grasp the depth of his hurt. She knew he had been somewhat bitter and angry with his father, but until today she had never guessed it went so deep. Nothing she said to Tyler seemed to help, so she just stopped talking and tried to listen. Left with his thoughts, Tyler struggled against the memories of his father's criticism. But now he was beginning to turn the anger against himself. He was the failure his dad had predicted he would be. He decided he needed to talk with someone or he was going to self-destruct.

The Problem Side of Anger

Tyler had done what many of us do with deep-seated anger. Sensing that we cannot do anything to change the circumstances, we redirect the energy associated with that anger in some way. It's called sublimation. Wives who are angry with their husbands and believe they cannot do anything about it may redirect the energy of their anger to go shopping and spend a lot. Or maybe they furiously clean what is already clean. A friend told me that his grandfather had once said to him that whenever he saw his wife, my friend's grandmother, polishing the silverware, he knew Grandma was upset about something.

Even Martin Luther, the sixteenth-century reformer, said, "I find nothing that promotes work better than angry fervor.

For when I wish to compose, write, pray and preach well, I must be angry. It refreshes my entire system, my mind is sharpened, and all unpleasant thoughts and depression fade away."[1] We can use the energy of our anger in a situation to sharpen what we are doing. But it seems that the longer we hold on to the anger, the less sharpened our focus is going to be. Apparently that happened with Tyler. And over time, when we suppress our anger, it stops working. When we try to redirect our anger in a different, more constructive direction for a long period of time, the anger will eventually leak out in some way, as it did for Tyler.

Another thing we can do with deep-seated anger is to just push it down even deeper. This is called repression, and when we repress our anger, we are trying to deny its existence. Over time, this often leads to a passive-aggressive approach to life and to our relationships. We can be nice to someone we are angry with, but our "niceness" has a hook in it. That hook may be passivity, it may be sweetly expressed sarcasm, or it may be as simple as agreeing to do something for the person and then never doing it.

The third way we deal with this type of anger is to find a way to express it. We need to let it all out, and we tell ourselves we are just trying to be cathartic about our anger. We can do this in several ways. We may talk with a friend about what is making us angry, and as our friend agrees with us and also begins to get angry, we feel justified. But our anger has also grown larger. There is no catharsis, for we have only increased the intensity of our anger. The same is true if we express anger directly to the person with whom we are angry.

Usually that leads only to a shouting match, and now we have more to be angry about.

When my associates and I directed an inpatient hospital program, each of us would take turns leading a Bible study group, which would be followed by an extended process group. One of my sessions was on the question of anger. I would ask, "If the Bible says in Ephesians 4:26, 'Be angry, but do not sin in your anger,' what are the ways we can be angry and sin, and the ways we can be angry and not sin? How can we be responsible with our anger, and how can we act irresponsibly with our anger?"

We would have a lively discussion that always ended up with the same basic answers. Sinful anger, we decided, is one-sided. Either I care only about myself and verbally beat you up in my anger, or I care only about you and beat myself up verbally. Another option was to just deny my anger. Sinful anger always seems to focus on revenge, or the desire to get even. Sinful anger often cares only about being right. It only compounds the angry feelings—I become angrier because I feel justified in my anger. And unresolved sinful anger often ends up cutting off the other person from our lives. Sinful anger holds grudges.

On the other hand, the groups agreed that when we experience anger that isn't sinful, we act responsibly, and we care about both people involved. In my anger, I care both for myself and for the other person. I don't verbally beat the other person up, nor do I verbally beat myself up. Anger that is not sinful is also focused primarily on the present and what we are doing about the situation. It doesn't hold grudges. This kind of anger is concerned not with being right but with a sense of justice. And being angry responsibly always seeks reconciliation if it is possible.

Here are some passages to meditate on to see what the Bible says about anger:

The LORD passed in front of Moses, calling out,

> Yahweh! The LORD!
>> The God of compassion and mercy!
> I am slow to anger
>> and filled with unfailing love and faithfulness.[2]

> His anger lasts only a moment,
>> but his favor lasts a lifetime!
> Weeping may last through the night,
>> but joy comes with the morning.[3]

> The LORD is compassionate and merciful,
>> slow to get angry and filled with unfailing love.
> He will not constantly accuse us,
>> nor remain angry forever.[4]

> Control your temper,
>> for anger labels you a fool.[5]

> A gentle answer deflects anger,
>> but harsh words make tempers flare.[6]

> Sensible people control their temper;
>> they earn respect by overlooking wrongs.[7]

> An angry person starts fights;
>> a hot-tempered person commits all kinds
>> of sin.[8]

Never pay back evil with more evil. Do things in such a way that everyone can see you are honorable. Do all that you can to live in peace with everyone.

Dear friends, never take revenge. Leave that to the righteous anger of God. For the Scriptures say,

> "I will take revenge;
>> I will pay them back,"
> says the LORD.[9]

Understand this, my dear brothers and sisters: You must all be quick to listen, slow to speak, and slow to get angry. Human anger does not produce the righteousness God desires. So get rid of all the filth and evil in your lives, and humbly accept the word God has planted in your hearts, for it has the power to save your souls.[10]

> Stop being angry!
>> Turn from your rage!
> Do not lose your temper—
>> it only leads to harm.[11]

"Don't sin by letting anger control you." Don't let the sun go down while you are still angry, for anger gives a foothold to the devil.[12]

Where Anger Takes Us

When we repress, suppress, or express our anger, it doesn't get resolved. It won't just go away, even though we may think that it does. But anger can take us to places we really don't want to go. Anger that festers at any level eventually turns into bitterness and resentment. And when this happens, we are in danger not just spiritually, but our health will be compromised as well.

Early studies attempted to differentiate anger from fear. Initially, researchers thought they had found a difference. The experiments couldn't create intense fear, but they could create intense anger. Eventually researchers discovered that the difference was based on the intensity of the two emotions. When they were able to create fear at an intensity equal to the intensity of the anger, there was no longer any difference between the two emotions. The truth is our brain reacts the same whether we feel fear or anger.

When the amygdala sends its messages, blood is taken from our organs and sent to our extremities in order to prepare us. If we are angry, we are being prepared to fight, not to take flight. Cortisol, adrenaline, histamines, and other hormones are released into the blood to prepare us to attack what appears to be threatening to us.

Here's an example of why the reactions are the same physiologically. Imagine that you are visiting a friend who has a ministry in the inner city. She lives in a neighborhood that, unless God called you to live there, would not be a place you would choose to live. As you finish dinner, your friend remembers she has a board meeting that night, so she suggests you go sightseeing downtown. "Just be back before 11:00 and you'll be safe," she says. "Nothing bad happens around here until after midnight."

You get back to her place a little after 11:00 and have to park your rental car several blocks away from your friend's apartment. You say goodbye to the car, assuming it will be stolen by morning. As you begin to walk the two long blocks to your friend's apartment, you suddenly hear footsteps behind you. You speed up; they speed up. You're too afraid to look behind you, so you start running. The footsteps start running as well, and now you're really afraid, but at this point you're close to the apartment.

Just as you get the key into the lock, the footsteps stop behind you and your friend says, "It's just me!" Now what do you feel? What had been intense fear just seconds earlier suddenly turns into intense anger at the "joke" that your now former friend has played on you. How long did it take for the fear to become anger? A microsecond. What changed? Nothing in your body. What changed was your perception of the threat. What had been extremely frightening for you was no longer a dangerous threat. So whether you feel anger or fear in a given situation will be mitigated by your *perception* of the threat.

People who live a fear-based life see themselves as basically helpless in most situations. A fear-based lifestyle was programmed into their subconscious as a child, as their experiences taught them to be afraid. People who live with a belligerent attitude, as if they have a chip on their shoulder, also have a subconscious that was programmed that way as a child. They learned through their experiences to falsely perceive themselves as more than able to handle any threat that comes their way.

How we deal with either fear or anger is all a matter of perception. It is not based on any difference biochemically in our brain or in our body. I feel fear when the threat appears to be bigger than me; I feel anger when it appears to me that I am bigger or stronger than the threat. And our basic perception was fixed in our subconscious mind by the time we were six or seven years old.

Now, if we live as if we have a chip on our shoulder, the real danger we face is expressed in Hebrews 12:15: "Look after each other so that none of you fails to receive the grace of God. Watch out that no poisonous root of bitterness grows up to trouble you, corrupting many." Where does this poisonous root of bitterness come from? How can a root of bitterness grow in us? Obviously, from unresolved anger that we hold on to in some way. Bitterness is an attitude of prolonged, intense anger. It leads to resentments and to an obsession that won't let go of grudges.

As the root of bitterness grows in us, we can become hostile to others, not just to the person who hurt us. We make unkind remarks, are sarcastic, and push others away. As a result, a spirit of bitterness leads us to end up feeling alone, isolated, and misunderstood. A vicious cycle takes place that leads to more anger and increased bitterness.

Years ago I read a book titled *Anger Kills*, written by a medical doctor.[13] His views were controversial at the time but have since been proven by brain research. He estimated that 95 percent of all terminal diseases have unresolved anger at their beginning. He said that the early cause of 95 percent of cancers, heart attacks, and other terminal diseases was unresolved anger. Time has proven him correct. That's why God had the writer of Hebrews give us such a strong warning.

The Bible gives us a clear example of the consequences of unresolved anger that turns into bitterness and an obsession with revenge. In the book of Esther, we meet a man named Haman. He was a government official who was enraged when he did not get homage from a Jewish exile named Mordecai. Haman's anger became bitterness. He concocted a plan not only to get rid of Mordecai but also for the mass murder of the Jewish people. He even had a huge gallows built on which he was going to have Mordecai hanged. But it all backfired on Haman, and instead of Mordecai hanging on the gallows, it was Haman.

Another passage to meditate on because it fits the Haman story so well is Paul's instruction to "get rid of all bitterness, rage, anger, harsh words, and slander, as well as all types of evil behavior. Instead, be kind to each other, tenderhearted, forgiving one another, just as God through Christ has forgiven you" (Eph. 4:31–32). Paul knew that the person who persists in bitterness may feel some passing pleasure in having a get-even mind-set. But the cost of bitterness is heavy, is self-defeating, and can be fatal. You don't destroy the other person with your bitterness—you really end up destroying yourself.

The Role of Forgiveness

In the passage we just quoted, Paul gives us the antidote to the root of bitterness. In place of bitterness, rage, and anger, we are called to forgive. Anger and bitterness kill; forgiveness heals. In spite of that truth, I've talked with many people who stubbornly refuse to forgive something or someone in their past. That raises the question of who it is that benefits from forgiveness.

I remember talking to a lady in my office who had deep resentment toward her father and was really struggling with the anger and hurt she felt over his cruel treatment of her during her childhood years. After several sessions, I brought up the fact that in order for her to experience healing of the anger and resentment she was experiencing, she would eventually be called upon to forgive her father.

I'll never forget her reaction. She jumped up from the couch and shouted, "Forgive? I'll never forgive that man!" I told her to relax, that I was not talking about her doing it right then but someday. When she calmed down, she went on to tell me again that her father had never ever said he was sorry for how he treated her, and in fact, he had never admitted to even one of the things she had tried to talk to him about over the years. She said she would never want to give him the benefit of knowing that she had forgiven him. She was punishing him by not forgiving him. What was she to do?

What she didn't realize was that she was stuck until she reached a point where she could begin the process of forgiveness. Her father did not have to be involved. She had to hear that she could, with God's help, forgive this man she had resented and hated for so many years.

Her question was, can a person forgive another who has hurt them without the other person being sorry or even admitting their wrong? Don't they need to suffer too? If they are not held accountable for what they did, isn't forgiveness a benefit to them?

But who really benefits from the act of forgiveness? The forgiver does! We might even say that forgiveness is a somewhat selfish act. When we forgive, we are the ones who become free from our anger. We benefit, not the offender. In some cases there is some benefit to the offender—when they know they have been forgiven, it may trigger in them the need to repent. But usually that's not the case. The offender may just go on their merry way in life, never dealing with those they have hurt. And we are often left with the anger and hurt until we begin to realize that we can act—we are the ones who can experience freedom by forgiving that person. In fact, we can forgive without even telling the other person. I can even forgive a parent or another person who has already died without knowing if they repented of what they did. I can forgive and never be reconciled with that one who hurt me.

If forgiveness heals and is the answer to our anger and pain, we can eventually get free of them and learn how to live a forgiving lifestyle. So if I don't need the offender's participation in my forgiveness of them and I may never reconcile with them, why is there so much emphasis on reconciliation in God's Word?

To understand this, we have to differentiate between forgiveness and reconciliation. They are two different processes. I can forgive and never be reconciled. And I can forgive and be reconciled, if there is godly sorrow and repentance on the part of the other person. Reconciliation always requires forgiveness on our part and genuine, godly sorrow—repentance—on the other person's part. Repentance is always necessary for there to be genuine reconciliation between two people.

The Jewish rabbis did, and still do, combine forgiveness with reconciliation. They were taught by their elders and teach that one can only forgive when the other person repents. If the offender does not repent or if they have already died, then we are free—we don't have the need or even the right to forgive if there is no sorrow expressed on the part of the offender.

Jesus taught a radically different model of forgiveness, even though as a boy he was taught the rabbis' model. Jesus's model separates forgiveness from reconciliation.

Look at the biblical model for conflict. If you have offended someone, Jesus says if "you are presenting a sacrifice at the altar in the Temple and you suddenly remember that *someone has something against you*, leave your sacrifice there at the altar. Go and be reconciled to that person. Then come and offer your sacrifice to God" (Matt. 5:23–24, italics mine). I've had people show me that passage to prove that forgiveness and reconciliation have to go together. But I point out the difference. This passage refers to the offender—the one who needs to repent. It instructs the offender to go and make things right—to repent. That can lead to reconciliation if the offended person has truly forgiven.

The principle for the offended person is highlighted in the Lord's Prayer, where Jesus tells us to pray to the Father to "forgive us our sins, as we have forgiven those who sin against us" (Matt. 6:12). Nothing is said here about the other person needing to repent.

In fact, in Matthew 18, Jesus tells us what to do when someone has hurt us: "If another believer sins against you, go privately and point out the offense" (v. 15). Begin with a gentle confrontation that gives the offending person the opportunity to make amends—to repent.

Jesus continues, "If the other person listens and confesses it, you have won that person back. But if you are unsuccessful, take one or two others with you and go back again, so that everything you say may be confirmed by two or three witnesses" (v. 16).

Then Jesus raises the consequences in his third step: "If the person still refuses to listen, take your case to the church" (v. 17). He finishes by telling us to wash our hands of the matter—in other words, if there is no repentance, we are to forgive and move on. We don't typically take the matter these days to the church, so this third step is seldom used unless it involves a pastor or a church leader.

Why do I say this passage is about forgiveness? Because right after Jesus outlines this process for us, he continues with a conversation with Peter about forgiveness, and then a long parable teaching on the consequences of unforgiveness.

In the parable, Jesus describes a servant who owes his king millions of dollars. It was a debt the man couldn't pay, so the king ordered that he and his family all be sold into slavery. The man begs the king, saying, "Please, be patient with me, and I will pay it all." The king saw the absurdity of the debt the man owed—he couldn't pay it in a dozen lifetimes—so the king took pity on him and forgave the debt.

Well, the man should have left the presence of his master feeling elated. His net worth had just reversed itself. His debt was canceled! But not this servant. He suddenly remembered another servant who owed him a couple thousand dollars, and he wanted payment—now!

It's always been interesting to me that this servant said the same words that the man had just said to the king—"Be patient with me, and I will pay it"—but the unforgiving man wouldn't wait and threw the servant into prison.

Fortunately, there were witnesses who were appalled by this man's greed and reported what had happened to the king. In anger, the king called the man back into his accounting room. He called him "you evil servant" and put him in debtors' prison until he could pay an unpayable debt.

The meaning of the parable transfers to us. We are that servant. We have been forgiven an unpayable debt by God through the sacrifice of Jesus. How dare we not be forgiving of ourselves and others!

After he finishes the story, I picture Jesus looking at his audience and maybe even pointing at them around the circle as he says, "That's what my heavenly Father will do to you if you refuse to forgive your brothers and sisters from your heart." For us today, forgiving others isn't an option—we've been forgiven so much by God.

Forgiveness in Jesus's story is the canceling of a debt. Even today, when a bank cancels an uncollectable loan, they refer to the loan as having been forgiven. I'm not certain what the accounting principle is that benefits the bank when they forgive a loan, but I am convinced they wouldn't forgive the loan unless it in some way affected their bottom line.

In the same way, when I forgive something that someone has done to me—a sin against me—I am the one who benefits from that forgiveness. I don't even need to tell the other person that I've forgiven them. What if I am resolving an issue in my mind with someone who has died and I want to forgive them? If forgiveness required both of us to participate, I would be in danger of being disobedient. So when I forgive, it is unilateral. I can do it all by myself. I am canceling a debt—the other person now owes me nothing.

To get these principles deep within your soul, take some time to meditate on the following passages related to forgiveness as the antidote to unresolved anger:

The Lord is slow to anger and filled with unfailing love, forgiving every kind of sin and rebellion.[14]

> And forgive us our sins,
>> as we have forgiven those who sin against
>> us. . . .

If you forgive those who sin against you, your heavenly Father will forgive you.[15]

Peter came to him and asked, "Lord, how often should I forgive someone who sins against me? Seven times?"

"No, not seven times," Jesus replied, "but seventy times seven!"[16]

You were dead because of your sins and because your sinful nature was not yet cut away. Then God made you alive with Christ, for he forgave all our sins. He canceled the record of the charges against us and took it away by nailing it to the cross.[17]

When you are praying, first forgive anyone you are holding a grudge against, so that your Father in heaven will forgive your sins, too.[18]

Get rid of all bitterness, rage, anger, harsh words, and slander, as well as all types of evil behavior. Instead, be kind to each other, tenderhearted, forgiving one another, just as God through Christ has forgiven you.[19]

Where Forgiveness Takes Us

Since forgiveness is basically a selfish act in that it sets me free from the unpayable debts owed to me from my past, there are benefits we can experience when we practice forgiveness. Think of what happens to us when we forgive someone, even someone who doesn't even care about being forgiven. Prior to my forgiving, I may have brooded over the offense. I nurse my hurt and anger toward that person. I may even be angry at myself for putting myself into that situation. Then, as I brood over my hurt and anger, I start to think about revenge. My thinking about revenge may feel good in the moment, but if I seek revenge, I have only made a bad situation worse.

In all likelihood, I will try to make certain I avoid that person who hurt me. If they go to my church, I will park away from where they do and sit in a different part of the sanctuary than they do. I am in danger of becoming obsessed with what happened, and my anger and hurt gradually begin to lay down the roots of bitterness.

Now think about what happens when I forgive that person from my heart. I am free of my anger, although I may still feel some hurt and disappointment. But I no longer think about revenge. In fact, I may even at some point actually pray good things for that person. Most of all, I am free emotionally from that past event. I may still be careful around that person because I don't really trust them, but I no longer have a need to avoid them.

There are two additional benefits, or gifts we give ourselves, when we overcome our anger with a spirit of genuine forgiveness. First, we are now free to experience God's peace within us. When Isaiah prophesied about the coming of Jesus as Messiah, he said he would be called "Wonderful Counselor, Mighty God, Everlasting Father, Prince of Peace" (Isa. 9:6). Later on in Isaiah, we read, "How beautiful on the mountains are the feet of the messenger who brings good news, the good news of peace and salvation" (Isa. 52:7). Here, salvation is coupled with the good news of peace!

The other gift we give ourselves is a spirit of gratitude. Our response to God's peace within us is a thankful heart. We can't be angry and bitter and at the same time experience a thankful heart. They are incompatible. Both Paul and James encourage us that, in spite of circumstances, we can experience peace and joy. Paul writes, "We can rejoice, too, when we run into problems and trials" (Rom. 5:3). And James tells us, "When troubles come your way, consider it an opportunity for great joy" (James 1:2).

Now, some have said that we are to rejoice about the problem—that when trouble hits, we are to ignore the frustration and be happy about the problem. I don't think that is either Paul's or James's point. Note that James says trouble gives us an *opportunity*. For what? To learn or discover in the process God's peace. He will carry us through the problems, and the joy we experience is that with God's help we are going to have a stronger faith on the other side of the problem. (We'll look at this more in chapter 10.)

Paul's letter to the Philippians is an example. Paul was writing from prison, and over and over he tells his readers to rejoice. For example, in Philippians 4:4, he writes, "Always be full of joy in the Lord. I say it again—rejoice!" Our joy is in the Lord, he says. It's not in the problem. Then Paul continues with the secret of joy. It's based on giving up worrying and instead praying about everything. And it is based on thinking right thoughts—thoughts about what is true, honorable, right, pure, lovely, excellent, and worthy of praise. When we do that, God's peace will fill our hearts, and we will live a life of gratitude and thankfulness.

Here are suggested passages to meditate on related to experiencing God's peace and developing a spirit of gratitude:

> God blesses those who work for peace,
>> for they will be called the children of God.[20]

Therefore, since we have been made right in God's sight by faith, we have peace with God because of what Jesus Christ our Lord has done for us.[21]

I pray that God, the source of hope, will fill you completely with joy and peace because you trust in him. Then you will overflow with confident hope through the power of the Holy Spirit.[22]

For God is not a God of disorder but of peace, as in all the meetings of God's holy people.[23]

Dear brothers and sisters, I close my letter with these last words: Be joyful. Grow to maturity. Encourage each other. Live in harmony and peace. Then the God of love and peace will be with you.[24]

Don't worry about anything; instead, pray about everything. Tell God what you need, and thank him for all he has done. Then you will experience God's peace, which exceeds anything we can understand. His peace will guard your hearts and minds as you live in Christ Jesus.

And now, dear brothers and sisters, one final thing. Fix your thoughts on what is true, and honorable, and right, and pure, and lovely, and admirable. Think about things that are excellent and worthy of praise. Keep putting into practice all you learned and received from me—everything you heard from me and saw me doing. Then the God of peace will be with you.[25]

Let the peace that comes from Christ rule in your hearts. For as members of one body you are called to live in peace. And always be thankful.[26]

As you move from anger and bitterness to a place of peace and gratitude, a key part of that movement is a spirit of willingness. It may seem like a tall order to break the pattern of anger, just as it is with fear. As you fill your soul with meditating on God's Word, he will remove your old resentments. He will help you forgive, even when the hurt goes deep within. A benefit of your salvation is God's desire for you to live at peace within yourself, with others, and with God himself. He is more than ready to help as you allow his Word to penetrate deep within the center of your being—your heart.

7

Moving from Loneliness
to Connection

John grew up in a large extended family in the Midwest. In their small town in Nebraska, there was always some family event that brought everyone together. If it wasn't the birth of a new niece or nephew, a graduation, or a wedding, there was some other reason for people to be together. John said he always felt like an observer—he didn't really enjoy the togetherness.

When he graduated from college, he couldn't wait to strike out on his own. He got a nice position with a public relations firm in Los Angeles and enjoyed the change of scenery. He even liked his work. He started to meet some interesting people, but his relationships never went beyond the work setting. He called home, as he said, "maybe once a month whether I needed to talk or not."

He eventually found that he couldn't stand his apartment. He didn't have a roommate—he said he didn't need one. But being alone started to drive him crazy. To break the monotony, he started sitting in a local pub, where he did as he had done with his family—he just watched people, seldom talking with anyone. Eventually a few of the regulars started to recognize him as a "new regular." Some of them tried talking with him, but John wasn't good at idle conversations, so eventually the other people let him enjoy his solitude.

Over time, John realized that if anyone around him had a cold or the flu, he ended up with it too. He wondered if it had something to do with his not sleeping that well. Oh, he'd get in his seven and a half to eight hours, but he felt like he was always tired. Maybe it had something to do with the twenty pounds he had put on since coming to LA. But when he got into a big argument with his neighbor, he decided it was time to get some help—things weren't going the way he expected.

When he arrived in my office, he didn't use the word *lonely*. He simply said that he was miserable. I asked him if he missed his family, and he quickly said that wasn't an issue for him. He loved being in LA. When we got to the subject of friends, he drew a blank. He had a lot of business acquaintances, but no one he could really call a friend.

"Part of it is by my own design," he said. "I've always seen myself as a loner. I don't really need people. At least that's what I thought. But man, I think I'm just so lonely!" he finally blurted out.

Everyone feels the effects of loneliness at times, but not to the same intensity John was experiencing. For most of us, it's usually temporary and is related to some loss that has occurred in our life, like losing a close friend or family member. It may last only a short time, or it may come and go. But that wasn't the case for John. For him, loneliness had become a miserable way of life.

Unfortunately, John and others who struggle with loneliness are not alone. Studies show that "about twenty percent of individuals—that would be sixty million people in the United States alone—feel sufficiently isolated for it to be a major source of unhappiness in their lives."[1] Living isolated lives is more the consequence of loneliness, as we will see, than it is a cause. Multiple studies show that typically people who report they are lonely are in contact with more people over a given period of time than those who say loneliness isn't an issue with them.

All humans are created to be in relationship. We are designed to connect with other people. The most emotionally charged events in our lives—when someone is born, when someone is married, or when someone dies—are all relational events!

However, it seems more and more people are accepting a lifestyle that is increasingly isolated from other people. In 1985, a survey asked people if they had someone with whom they could discuss important matters. When the study was repeated in 2004, three times as many people said they had no one with whom they could talk. Our increasing propensity to live an isolated life will compound the problem of loneliness in the coming years.

Who Gets Lonely?

Loneliness has nothing to do with solitude, nor does it relate to being an introvert. Researcher John Cacioppo has found that there are three factors that contribute to the chronic experience of loneliness. The first factor has to do with our vulnerability to the experience of social disconnection—it's part of our genetic makeup, as well as how our environment has affected our genes. Some of us have a greater need than others to be included in social settings. Just like we have different abilities to tolerate physical pain, we have different abilities to tolerate the pain of social exclusion.

Second, we also differ in our ability to regulate our emotions related to being isolated. It's not just our surface reactions to being isolated but, more importantly, what is going on deep inside of us about it.

And third, the experience of loneliness is directly related to how we frame our experiences of isolation. We look to causes and are most times off base as to why we feel lonely. Our ability to properly frame our experience will greatly diminish over time the more we experience loneliness.[2]

These three factors are all interdependent—they each affect our ability to handle the other factors. One thread that runs through all three is that we need to be less distracted by our own thoughts and feelings if we are to be unaffected by the experience of isolation or the early stages of feeling lonely. Over time, the growing feeling of loneliness will change our cognitive appraisal of being alone and feed into the experience of loneliness.

These are the factors that lead to a life of loneliness, but there is no specific group of people who is prone to loneliness. Almost thirty million people live alone in the United States, a large number of them over sixty-five, but that does not sentence them to a struggle with loneliness, regardless of their age. Many do fine living alone and do not report themselves lonely at all. In addition, lonely people are no more stressed by life's circumstances than non-lonely people. But they do experience more divorces, more run-ins with neighbors, and more estrangement from their family. Like John, they also gain weight, have a lowered immune system, and don't sleep very well. So obviously, something is going on in the chronically lonely that is different from those who don't report being lonely.

The Brain of the Lonely Person

A baby's brain at birth has over two hundred billion neurons. Gradually, about half of the neurons will die so that as the infant becomes an adult, they will end up with around one hundred billion neurons in the brain. What happened to the others? Basically, the neurons that thrive into adulthood are the ones that connected with other neurons. Those that died didn't connect.

I remember seeing a booklet years ago with the title *Wired to Connect*. It was a promotion for some group activity, and at the time, it didn't make a lot of sense to me. I didn't understand how true that statement was until I better understood how our brain functions. Just like the neurons in the brain, we are created for connection with others.

So does that mean chronic loneliness, chronic lack of connection, is unhealthy? Definitely. Research has shown that lonely people suffer significantly more from high blood pressure, immunity issues, and various cardiovascular ailments. People who suffer from loneliness will age more quickly than someone who is not lonely. Their health issues will be the same as those of a non-lonely person who never exercises or who is obese, and they will have just as high a risk of fatal illnesses as a lifetime smoker. Their health issues are not caused by the fact that they are alone. They are based purely on the subjective experience of being chronically lonely.

The genetic information in their cells is part of the problem, but it is the overlay of a person's experiences and environment that either turns on a specific gene or turns it off. So our genes alone do not shape us. Our epigenetic experiences—our life experiences and environment—do as well. If we are wired to connect, just like our brain neurons do, then when we disconnect and experience chronic loneliness, we are not living the way God designed us to live.

How do our life experiences and environment feed into our loneliness? By affecting the chemistry of the brain. And our brain chemistry affects what happens with our genes. One of the hormones released under the stress of loneliness is epinephrine, which tends to arouse us. But it also increases our experience of frustration and emotional pain. The more stressed we are, the more epinephrine is released into our system. Cortisol is also available in abundance in our system. These both will affect in a negative way the genetic expression in our body.

What we lack when we continually experience loneliness is oxytocin, the comfort and connecting hormone. Without connection with another person in our life, our output of oxytocin is limited. We can get some released into our system by eating, but its primary release mechanism comes when we connect in a deeper way with another person.

Studies have shown that when a mother breast-feeds her baby, oxytocin is released both in the baby and in the mother. The mother-baby bond is built around the mutual release of oxytocin into their systems. When a nursing mother sees her baby, oxytocin will begin to be released, which will then hasten the increase of milk to be made available to the baby. Oxytocin is also a calming hormone that allows us to better regulate our emotional reaction to our experiences—in particular, in this chapter, the experience of feeling isolated.

Serotonin is another brain substance that is related to comfort and to the elevation of our mood. It's interesting, though, that too much serotonin works the opposite way and sends us into a state of despair. The balance of all of these brain substances causes certain genes to activate and others to shut down. And they provide either higher anxiety or calm and comfort.

These chemicals especially affect the amygdala—our brain's warning system. They also affect the hippocampus and other regions in the brain that help us connect with other people. There is a region in the brain called the *dorsal anterior cingulate cortex*. When we experience physical pain, that part of the brain registers the pain and allows us to experience it. What researchers have found is that the pain of loneliness is registered in that same part of the brain. This means that we experience the emotional pain of loneliness in the same way we would experience physical pain. This is why it is so difficult to escape from the reality and pain of loneliness. It is the same deeply disruptive hurt as breaking a bone in our body!

Loneliness or Depression

It's all too easy to lump together loneliness with being depressed. Those who experience loneliness over time usually end up also being depressed. But loneliness and depression are different in important ways. One way that Cacioppo differentiates between the two is to point out that in many ways they are even opposites.[3] One important difference is that in the early stages, the feeling of loneliness is a warning, like hunger. It is saying that something basic to life is missing. There is a need to connect with someone. But that warning is also threatening, for the experience of the lonely person is that connection can be painful, even more painful than the loneliness. So there is an interior conflict involved. Part of the lonely person wants to move toward other people and connect, but another part is terrified of being hurt again, so they withdraw.

Depression doesn't have this conflict of movement. It is basically a shutting down emotionally. When I am depressed, I am depressed in every way. It's pervasive throughout every part of my life. When I am lonely, I am struggling with relationships, but I may still be coping satisfactorily in the other parts of my life.

Depression is not only all-pervasive, it also doesn't go anywhere. But there is movement in loneliness, at least in the earlier stages. I want to reach out—I may even reach out tentatively. But when I don't get the response I wish for—which I probably expected anyway—I withdraw. With depression, I am stuck. I don't reach out to anyone.

Eventually the two will come together. The longer I live in my loneliness, the more likely I am to become depressed. Eventually, other symptoms appear, marking my struggle with loneliness. I become increasingly shy, my self-esteem suffers, I feel more anxiety, and I become more pessimistic and hostile. I'm less agreeable with others, partly out of my fear of their negative evaluation. And in the end both depression and loneliness make me feel trapped—I am immobilized, and it feels like there is nothing I can do about it.

But remember, connection is the answer.

The Role of Attachment

One of the early studies, and one of the most referenced studies on connection, was done by Harry Harlow in 1958. He took newborn rhesus monkeys away from their mothers and gave them two artificial surrogate mothers. One was made only of wire but had a feeding tube available. The other was also made of wire but was covered with a soft cloth.

Sometimes it had food available as well. But regardless of which "mother" provided food, the infant monkeys preferred the mother covered with the soft cloth. When they were startled or were upset, they ran to the soft mother.

He also studied what would happen if the newborns only had the wire mother available. They would be fed, but there was no comforting connection available to them. Later, when these monkeys rejoined the large group of monkeys, either they were too aggressive in playing with the other infant monkeys, or more likely they simply isolated themselves from the others. Either way, they were socially unable to connect with any of the other monkeys.

Another landmark study was the work done by Austrian scientist Konrad Lorenz. He studied animal behavior, and his experiment called for him to be the first living being present when a brood of baby geese broke out of their eggs. Instead of imprinting and attaching to the mother goose, they imprinted on Lorenz, who became the mother figure to these baby geese. His study is famous for the photos of the scientist walking around being followed by "his" brood of goslings.

Part of Lorenz's experiment required him to teach his brood what they needed to know to survive in the wild. But his study was a major part of the groundwork that led to the understanding of attachment and the work of John Bowlby.

John Bowlby developed a theory of attachment that differentiated the several ways we as humans connect in the first year of our life with our mother and father. The way we connect in that first year eventually explains how we connect with other people as we mature into adulthood.

Bowlby built his theory around what he observed in toddlers, particularly what happened when mothers brought their toddlers to the park to play. If a child had what he eventually called a "secure attachment," the child would feel free enough to leave his "secure base"—his mother—and explore the exciting world around him in the park. If he got a little too far from his mother or became fearful, he would come back to her. It was like he returned to his secure base. Then, as his feeling of safety returned, he would again venture out to explore this interesting world. His mother had been a refuge for the child to retreat to—he reconnected with her—and that made him feel safe enough to go back out again and play.

As adults, people with a secure attachment typically have healthy connections and meaningful relationships. Apart from experiencing a trauma as they grow up, they will probably not struggle with the chronic experience of loneliness. They learned during that first year of life what connection was all about. Their bond with their mother gave them the assurance she would be there if needed.

But Bowlby also saw two other patterns. One he called the "avoidant attachment." He described this as what happened when a child did not really feel like he had a secure base. He had learned that his mother would not be there for him if he needed her. So he created his own secure base within himself. He would set off to play and appear to be fearless in his behavior. He would go off exploring, and the presence of his mother was not a factor. He acted as if he were self-sufficient. When this child grows up, he will become a self-sufficient adult, not feeling like he really needs other people. He is the epitome of the lone cowboy riding off into the sunset.

Adults who were avoidantly attached as children would probably say that they seldom feel lonely. But if they were to slow down and reflect on specific situations, the feeling of chronic loneliness might well come to the surface. Statements such as "Nobody really cares about me, but that's okay" would begin to unmask their lack of comfort with their aloneness.

The third pattern Bowlby saw was what he called the "anxious attachment." These were the kids that he theorized didn't fully trust their secure base to be secure. Mom wasn't dependable, so they seemed very insecure and stayed close to her, sometimes even clinging to her. If another child came to play, these children might turn away and crawl up on their mother's lap. Children with this attachment style were anxious about their relationships, always fearing that the important people in their life might leave them. As adults, they were the ones who would most likely experience chronic loneliness.

Mary Ainsworth, who was a student of Bowlby, identified a fourth attachment style in her subsequent research. She called it the "fearful attachment." These were children who were physically and emotionally abused. They weren't certain if their base was safe or if she would turn on them and attack them. They didn't know how to approach their mother. They didn't know whether they would get a welcoming hug or a slap in the face for bothering her. Adults with this attachment style would certainly be clear about their constant feelings of loneliness.

Breaking the Loneliness Cycle

So does our attachment style determine the outcome of our struggle with loneliness? Not entirely. It may give us insight into some of the roots of our loneliness. God created each of us for relationship, regardless of our past. Therefore, he wants all of us to experience connection with others. In fact, he promises it. Look at what David wrote in Psalm 68:4–6:

> Sing praises to God and to his name!
> > Sing loud praises to him who rides the clouds.
> His name is the LORD—
> > rejoice in his presence!
> Father to the fatherless, defender of widows—
> > that is God, whose dwelling is holy.
> God places the lonely in families;
> > he sets the prisoners free and gives them joy.

This is a passage that everyone who struggles with loneliness can meditate on until it becomes a reality in their life. He—the God of the universe—will place the lonely in families. He—the God of the universe—will set the prisoner of loneliness free! When we meditate on these verses, we begin to understand God's concern for our loneliness. He wants us to understand that he is at work in us. When we step out in faith and risk forming social connections that are meaningful to us and to the other person, God is there with us.

Our first step in renewing our mind and heart is to understand what God has to say about connection. Our next step in that healing process is to meditate on what God wants us to know about our need to connect with other people. Begin your meditation with the Psalm 68 passage. Here are additional passages you can meditate on as well:

Owe nothing to anyone—except for your obligation to love one another. If you love your neighbor, you will fulfill the requirements of God's law. . . . Love does no wrong to others, so love fulfills the requirement of God's law.[4]

For you have been called to live in freedom, my brothers and sisters. But don't use your freedom to satisfy your sinful nature. Instead, use your freedom to serve one another in love. For the whole law can be summed up in this one command: "Love your neighbor as yourself."[5]

Is there any encouragement from belonging to Christ? Any comfort from his love? Any fellowship together in the Spirit? Are your hearts tender and compassionate? Then make me truly happy by agreeing wholeheartedly with each other, loving one another, and working together with one mind and purpose.

Don't be selfish; don't try to impress others. Be humble, thinking of others as better than yourselves. Don't look out only for your own interests, but take an interest in others, too.[6]

Let us think of ways to motivate one another to acts of love and good works. And let us not neglect our meeting together, as some people do, but encourage one another, especially now that the day of his return is drawing near.[7]

Most important of all, continue to show deep love for each other, for love covers a multitude of sins. Cheerfully share your home with those who need a meal or a place to stay.[8]

This is his commandment: We must believe in the name of his Son, Jesus Christ, and love one another.[9]

As we learn to meditate on what God wants us to experience, we have a solid foundation for the next task as God begins to change our hearts, renew our minds, and repair the roots of our loneliness. Our part of the healing process is to work on changing our thought patterns. In the past when we had a negative experience, our pattern was to withdraw and isolate. Not only do we frame that experience as negative, but we recall all the other negative experiences that are similar. Then we isolate and withdraw from social contacts.

Here's what non-lonely people do. When they have a negative experience in a relationship, they look at all the aspects of what happened. They look at what their part might have been, and then they think of all the possible explanations for the other person's behavior. They don't brood or withdraw or become negative. In fact, if the experience is serious enough, they may even share what happened with a positive-thinking friend who will help them put it in perspective.

At work, the non-lonely people work on forming good relationships with their co-workers. As they do this, they may find their own performance improving, which could lead to a promotion and increased income. In their social life, they have learned how to reframe negative experiences. They don't ignore them and let them fester inside; instead, they balance them with all the positive things that are happening around them. Even for those who are lonely, there are positive things going on around them. They just don't focus on the positive, choosing instead to focus primarily on the negative.

Another task in breaking the cycle of loneliness is to practice random acts of kindness. Non-lonely people have learned how to extend themselves to others. They may not feel like it at the moment, but they overcome that tendency to withdraw and lick their wounds. They may not do some huge thing—it may only be something very small. It may only be a smile, or it may be giving some change to the person in line in front of them at the grocery store to complete their purchase.

After the resurrection, Peter was probably feeling very much alone. Prior to the crucifixion, he had bragged about his loyalty to Jesus in front of the other disciples. They knew he had totally failed to live up to what he had said and, more importantly, Jesus knew it. Following the resurrection, in one of Jesus's appearances to the disciples, he prepared them a breakfast. Peter was one of the seven disciples there. After breakfast, Jesus asked Peter three times whether or not he loved him. And when Peter answered each question in the affirmative, Jesus gave him something to do. He told Peter, "Feed my sheep." The cycle of loneliness that could have taken over in Peter's life was broken by Jesus giving him something to do.

So you, the lonely, are being told to do something. Do random acts of kindness without expecting anything in return. In the morning when I walk my dog, I make it a point to smile and greet each person I meet. Sometimes they smile back and return the greeting; sometimes they ignore what I said and even ignore me. It doesn't matter. For me it is a small random act of kindness, and it feels good. And I don't expect anything in return.

What happens when we do these kind acts is that oxytocin is being released into our system. This surge of the comfort cocktail feels good to me, and that is reward enough to keep me doing it. For the lonely person, beginning to do these random acts with no expectation of return begins to break the negative cycle they are caught up in.

Scientists refer to what is called the butterfly effect. They say that the flutter of a butterfly's wings—say, in Africa—can set off a string of reactions that could eventually change the weather in Europe days or weeks later. That may sound hard to believe, but it is used as an illustration of how changing a little thing can set off a series of other events that eventually bring about major change. So no matter how small your effort might be, consider it to be the butterfly effect. Think of how a tiny effect can become a powerful force to begin change.

Taking It a Step Further

We've looked at what God wants us to understand about connection. We have outlined small ways a person experiencing loneliness can begin to break the cycle. Now we are ready for the next phase—the real work. Breaking the loneliness cycle requires just one other person with whom you are going to develop a friendship. Begin with an action plan. Think about what interests you. Are you interested in sports? Are you interested in the philharmonic? Do you love your church? Identify your interest and then begin small. Find one way to get involved with other people who are interested in what you're interested in.

Let's go back and look at how John broke his loneliness cycle. One of the things he said was that he loved music. He didn't play an instrument, but he loved orchestra music and knew the sound of every instrument. When he moved to LA, he settled in Orange County. He acknowledged that he had been fearful of the effect the change of location would have on him. He also admitted that he had always secretly struggled with feelings of loneliness. I suggested he begin to look for some ways to comfortably get involved with people who enjoyed music. I proposed he check to see if there were any volunteer groups connected to Orange County's Pacific Symphony. I know, we started big—there were smaller venues he could have checked out. But he found there was a charitable organization that supported the symphony. He made the contact and got involved. All along he was fairly consistent in meditating on the suggested Scriptures as well as additional passages unrelated to loneliness.

As John started to spend more time with the volunteer group, he consciously made the effort to extend himself to other people, and slowly he started to make some friends. As he did, he found that his feelings of loneliness were beginning to fade. Maybe the executive part of his brain began to push away the feelings of loneliness and started to reward the feelings of connection he was experiencing.

We also worked hard on strategies to help him choose the right kind of people in order to practice having a deeper connection. Who were the people similar to him? Who was responsive to his input? Who seemed to reach out to him? And then, as he stepped things up a bit, we looked at how he was going to regulate any negative responses or emotions he might experience. How was he going to stay calm in social situations that didn't appear to be going well? Gradually he found some people with whom he started to feel safe—safe enough that he could explore having deeper connections. He also discovered that some of the people volunteering with the orchestra charity also attended his church. They went to the front of his line as people he might be able to build a deeper connection with, especially since he was getting to know them in both settings.

We especially worked on strategies for managing his expectations. John said he thought he had a tendency to get ahead of himself in relationships. He would begin to expect more from other people than they were ready to give. So he worked hard at adjusting his expectations, and as he did, he found he wasn't so demanding in his mind about other people. He was learning to expect the best from someone else and not to be negative when what they offered fell short of what he expected.

The Power of a Volleyball

Many of us saw the movie *Cast Away*, in which Tom Hanks is stranded on an uncharted, uninhabited island. As time passed, he learned how to survive, but the loneliness was overpowering. When his plane crashed, he salvaged some of the packages, and in one he found a volleyball. He gave the volleyball a name—Wilson. He gradually built a relationship with Wilson. Now that he had a "friend," he didn't feel so alone. He talked often with Wilson, and over time he formed a strong attachment to his friend. In truth, his connection with Wilson was the only thing that gave him hope.

But eventually, Wilson was washed away in a storm—lost at sea. And Hanks's character was alone again. He grieved his lost friend. But fortunately, it wasn't too long after that he was rescued.

Wilson is an example of how we are wired to connect. God made us that way, and when we go against that design, we experience the debilitating effects of loneliness. But it doesn't have to be that way. Remember the promise that "God places the lonely in families." But we have to be open and do our part of the healing process as well.

8

Moving from Lust to Intimacy

This story and the process it describes are too common. Ron was a minister and the only pastor on the staff. The only other person on the church's payroll was a part-time secretary who was in the office in the mornings. Weekly church attendance averaged about 110 plus children, and there had been some moderate growth in those numbers over the two years Ron had been the pastor.

Most days, Ron spent the afternoons alone in the church. He always said he used that time for his sermon preparation. But it wasn't until his strange trip to St. Louis that his wife, Sarah, grew suspicious. He said he went there to talk with another church about a position. But for Sarah, something didn't add up. The trip had come out of the blue. Ron hadn't talked about any church move, and that added to Sarah's curiosity and suspicion.

She had never done it before, but suddenly she felt she needed to check both of his computers. His history on the computer at the church was erased, but it wasn't on his laptop at home. Sarah felt nauseated from the shock as she looked at some of the sites her husband had visited. In a panic, she tried to contact Ron on his cell phone, but there was no answer. So she decided to call the church's district superintendent (typically in their denomination called the "DS") for help on what to do next.

As she told him what she had found on Ron's computer, the DS was appalled. He asked to talk to Ron, but Sarah said he was out of town talking to another church. As they talked, he said he would contact the churches in that area to see who might have been talking to Ron. "But," he said, "I will be at the church office Tuesday morning to meet with you and Ron." Then he added, "I'll let him know I'm coming."

When Ron got home on Saturday, he knew something was up. Why did the DS want to meet with both of them, he wondered? At first he defended his reason for being away, but when Sarah showed him the history on his laptop, he was silent. He kept his silence through Sunday, even preached that morning. But by late afternoon, he finally admitted that he had gone to St. Louis to meet a woman and that he thought he was in love with her.

As the story unfolded, Sarah found out that Ron had not only been on all those porn sites, he had also participated in various sexually explicit chat rooms. That's where he seemed to hit it off with this other woman, and the two of them started chatting privately. Finally, she offered to pay for his airline ticket so they could meet, and they did.

Then Ron stopped talking again.

On Tuesday morning, the DS relieved Ron of his pastoral duties for an unspecified period of time and then referred him to me for counseling. Ron's returning to the pastorate was conditional on what happened in his counseling.

We started by looking at his history with pornography. It began one summer when a friend brought over to his house one of his father's *Playboy* magazines. Ron was eleven at the time. His friend had carefully hidden the magazine in his backpack, and he knew he had to replace it before his father came home from work. Ron was almost mesmerized by the pictures of the naked women—something he'd never seen before. A couple of days later, at that friend's house, he showed Ron how to find more pictures of naked women on the internet. From that time on, Ron said, he was hooked.

His dad caught him once on an internet porn site, but all he got from his father was a "spiritual lesson" on this forbidden activity. He was more careful to erase his history after that lecture. Ron thought some about what his father had said, but the pull to the porn sites was just too strong. Maybe he would be able to stop once he got married. But that only lasted a month or so. He did cut back on how much time he spent viewing the various sites when he started seminary. But the quiet afternoons in the church office were more than he could handle. His passion for pornography was back full bore.

We only met together two times, for Ron made it clear that he was in counseling only to mark time. He had already determined that he was going to give up the ministry, leave his wife and kids, and move to St. Louis. He didn't care, really. And that's what he did. That was the power of his addiction.

The World's Path—What's Happening to Our Culture

Pornography has always been around in some form. But today, pornography is big business. Worldwide, it brings in annually over one hundred billion dollars. The United States ranks fourth in the world behind China, South Korea, and Japan with revenues of over thirteen billion dollars.[1] That amount is larger than the combined income of all the professional football, baseball, and basketball franchises. It is larger than the combined revenues of ABC, CBS, and NBC.[2] Porn sites get more visitors each month than Netflix, Amazon, and Twitter combined. And one porn site has a bandwidth six times larger than Hulu, which carries most of our TV programs.[3] There are over twenty-four million pornographic websites, which amount to 12 percent of all the websites on the internet.[4] Over one hundred thousand websites offer child pornography, which is illegal in the United States. Representatives of the pornography industry told Congress in 2009 that 20 to 30 percent of the traffic on their sites comes from children. The largest group of children is those between ages twelve and seventeen.[5]

Some think pornography is exclusively a male domain. But one out of three visitors to all pornographic websites is a woman. Twenty percent of men admit to viewing pornography at work, and 13 percent of women admit to accessing pornography at work. Women more than men keep their pornography use a secret, and 17 percent of women admit to struggling with a pornography addiction.

Christians aren't exempt. Fifty-three percent of men who have attended Promise Keepers events admit to having viewed pornography during the previous week. Forty-seven percent of Christians say that pornography is an issue in their home. With the advent first of home video machines and then the development of the internet, "pornography today has become an accepted part of life for much of society,"[6] Christians included. These are statistics related to the hardcore pornographic industry. It doesn't include what is called "soft porn"—things like Victoria's Secret catalogs, certain television shows, and other similar highly suggestive magazines. The result is that pornography is readily available, it's affordable, and it allows the user to remain anonymous.

Studies show that women typically are not as oriented to the visual as men. But there is another form of pornography that attracts them. For a woman, it is much more tempting to get involved in reading sexually explicit romance novels. They're much more emotional.

At this time there are three novels in the Fifty Shades series. The first, *Fifty Shades of Grey*, was published in April 2012. Two more books in the series were released soon after. For months, the top three bestselling novels were the ones in this series. *Fifty Shades of Grey*, at the time of this writing in early 2013, is still one of the top ten fiction books. The series has been called "mommy porn," for the primary audience drawn to this trilogy is married women in their thirties. Teens and college-age women are not far behind.

This series of books highlights bondage, discipline, sadism, and masochistic sexual encounters (BDSM). It has been defended by feminists, some of whom say that its explicit sexual themes, women's open consumption of the books, and their sharing and discussion of its sexual content make it a feminist success. It's explicit enough that some public libraries have banned it from their shelves.

But the promise of pornography is a lie. The lie is that pornography will lead to sexual fulfillment. In an article published in *Psychotherapy Networker* in 2009, Wendy Maltz, a secular sex therapist, wrote about both her personal and professional experience with pornography. At age eleven, a neighbor girl showed her some pictures she had found in her grandfather's nightstand. They featured pretty women in frilly corsets with bare bottoms. She said she and her friend giggled as they looked at the images. But she also said that several of the images became locked in her brain. That was in the 1960s, before the pornography explosion.

She then described how, as a sex therapist beginning in the 1980s, she had used certain pornographic movies as an intervention in her practice. She typically suggested these movies to help women better understand their own sexuality. But she admitted to having some misgivings about using these films due to their depiction of multiple partners and extramarital sex.

Finally, in the 1990s, Maltz stopped using pornography. Her reasons were that the current titles available went far beyond the earlier films and caused many of her clients to protest. Many of them told her that viewing the films made them feel dirty and angry. They were turned off by the way pornography portrayed women. Finally, she asked herself, "How can I support something that portrays sex as a commodity, people as objects, and violence, humiliation, and recklessness as exciting? What am I doing encouraging people to condition their arousal to self-centered, sensually blunted, loveless sex?"[7] She was finished with pornography.

I tell her story because she does not base her protest about pornography on spiritual principles as I do. She began to see the destructive effect it had on her clients. She once was an advocate of its use but eventually saw through the lies.

Another writer, feminist Naomi Wolf, says that especially for men, our culture has been "pornographized." She goes on to add, "For most of human history, the erotic images have been reflections of, or celebrations of, or substitutes for, real naked women. For the first time in human history, the images' power and allure have supplanted that of real naked women. Today, real naked women are just bad porn."[8] I say, God knows best!

What Happens in Our Brain with Pornography

How can we call compulsive use of pornography an addiction? There is nothing being injected or ingested in our bodies. But research shows that like gambling, overeating, and shopping, the continued use of pornography leads to what is now called a "process addiction." In each of these process addictions, a person becomes addicted to a set of behaviors that powerfully alters their brain.

Whether it is a man who is stimulated by a visual image or a woman who is stimulated by the emotion contained in an erotic romance novel, neural pathways in the brain related to the sexual content become widened. As a person repeatedly reinforces these pathways, they become deeper and deeper. Eventually, pathways God intended for intimacy become overly sexualized.

In our brain, there is a reward system called the *ventral tegmental area*, or VTA. Its task is to manufacture the neurotransmitter dopamine and make it available to the body, especially to the brain. This happens in a number of different ways, like when we anticipate eating or drinking. It primarily responds to anything pleasurable, including our response to all addictive drugs. The brain chemistry of an orgasm in a man is the same as what a person using heroin or cocaine experiences. It is this response that leads to the process addiction.

When someone is viewing pornography, the hypothalamus and VTA activity are both elevated, which is what causes the pituitary to release dopamine. The anxiety and tension felt while a person is viewing pornography also increases the activity of the amygdala.

It appears that masturbation is the key in the addiction to pornography and sex. First the visual system is activated when a man looks at porn. Then the motor system and the sensory system are turned on through masturbation. Then the neurological system kicks in as the feeling of euphoria results from the release of oxytocin, vasopressin, and dopamine when he ejaculates. This is a bonding cocktail in the brain, as we saw in the previous chapter. Regardless of why the man views pornography, this neurological and neurochemical activation reinforces the addictive behaviors. The consequence of this neurological habit is that eventually the man bonds primarily to the images, and his bond to his wife, a real person, diminishes and, as in the case of Ron, disappears.

Research has also shown that when someone is involved in pornography, 42 percent of their partners say the use of pornography made them feel unsure and less attractive. Those feelings are compounded by the finding, according to another survey, that more than half of those involved with pornography have lost interest in sexual intercourse, and a third of their partners have also lost interest. Many of the men can't perform, which has helped lead to the popularity of Viagra and similar drugs for erectile dysfunction. In addition, 68 percent of divorce filings involve one party meeting a new lover over the internet. Fifty-six percent involve one party being obsessively interested in pornography. This is not the way God designed sex!

Not every man gets involved with pornography. But a common issue with men is where the problem usually begins—with lust. I'm often asked, "Is lust sin?" The typical answer is, "That depends on how long you look." Jesus did not treat lust lightly. If lust is an issue for you, one of the passages for you to meditate on is found in Matthew 5:27–30:

You have heard the commandment that says, "You must not commit adultery." But I say, anyone who even looks at a woman with lust has already committed adultery with her in his heart. So if your eye—even your good eye—causes you to lust, gouge it out and throw it away. It is better for you to lose one part of your body than for your whole body to be thrown into hell. And if your hand—even your stronger hand—causes you to sin, cut it off and throw it away. It is better for you to lose one part of your body than for your whole body to be thrown into hell.

These are harsh words from Jesus. But the harshness points out what Jesus considered to be an extreme danger, particularly in men—lust. In many men this problem is so frustrating that the thought of plucking out the eyes seems like an option.

Many men who come to my counseling office tell me about their battle with lust. One man told me of how he is winning that battle. He said that he had struggled all his teen and adult life with lustful thoughts when he encountered a beautiful woman. He said that a few years ago, he asked the Lord to give him insight into how he might get those thoughts under control. He began a regimen of memorizing Scripture and asked God to bring those passages to his mind when he started to have lustful thoughts. He said that was the beginning of a transformation in his life. He told of the incredible difference it has made in how he sees those women he considers beautiful. He has gradually changed his thought patterns and is convinced that it is really God who is transforming his mind.

Here are some additional verses to meditate on in dealing with lustful thoughts, or with a struggle with pornography or explicit romance novels:

> My son, obey your father's commands,
>> and don't neglect your mother's instruction. . . .
> It will keep you from the immoral woman,
>> from the smooth tongue of a promiscuous
>>> woman.
> Don't lust for her beauty.
>> Don't let her coy glances seduce you.
> For a prostitute will bring you to poverty,
>> but sleeping with another man's wife will cost
>>> you your life.
> Can a man scoop a flame into his lap
>> and not have his clothes catch on fire?
> Can he walk on hot coals
>> and not blister his feet?
> So it is with the man who sleeps with another
>> man's wife.
>> He who embraces her will not go unpunished.
>>>> Proverbs 6:20, 24–29

Here the writer of Proverbs talks about the prostitute. The word *pornography* is made up of two Greek words—*porne*, which can be translated as "female captives" or "prostitutes," and *graphia*, which refers to "writings." So it is the writings of prostitutes. Proverbs' reference to prostitutes certainly fits with pornography.

The word *porne* is often used in the form of *porneia*, which is translated as "fornication" or "sexual immorality." Paul uses this word in a number of places—in particular, in the following passages from 1 and 2 Corinthians. The culture of Corinth at the time of Paul was not unlike what we just described happening in our culture today. Sex, it seemed, was on everyone's mind. If this is your issue, begin by meditating on these verses:

> You say, "Food was made for the stomach, and the stomach for food." (This is true, though someday God will do away with both of them.) But you can't say that our bodies were made for sexual immorality. They were made for the Lord, and the Lord cares about our bodies.[9]

> Run from sexual sin! No other sin so clearly affects the body as this one does. For sexual immorality is a sin against your own body.[10]

> Because there is so much sexual immorality, each man should have his own wife, and each woman should have her own husband.[11]

> I am afraid that when I come again, God will humble me in your presence. And I will be grieved because many of you have not given up your old sins. You have not repented of your impurity, sexual immorality, and eagerness for lustful pleasure.[12]

Again, the words of Jesus:

> It is what comes from inside that defiles you. For from within, out of a person's heart, come evil thoughts, sexual

immorality, theft, murder, adultery, greed, wickedness, deceit, lustful desires, envy, slander, pride, and foolishness. All these vile things come from within; they are what defile you.[13]

Paul refers to the desires of our sinful nature and its resulting behaviors:

The results are very clear: sexual immorality, impurity, lustful pleasures, idolatry, sorcery, hostility, quarreling, jealousy, outbursts of anger, selfish ambition, dissension, division, envy, drunkenness, wild parties, and other sins like these. Let me tell you again, as I have before, that anyone living that sort of life will not inherit the Kingdom of God.[14]

So put to death the sinful, earthly things lurking within you. Have nothing to do with sexual immorality, impurity, lust, and evil desires. . . . Because of these sins, the anger of God is coming.[15]

Paul also instructs his young pastoral protégé, Timothy:

Run from anything that stimulates youthful lusts. Instead, pursue righteous living, faithfulness, love, and peace.[16]

Both Jesus and Paul contrast a life that involves unbridled lust and the immorality of pornography with a life of purity and righteous living, but God's path takes us on a much bigger journey. His path is designed to take us where our sexuality was meant to lead us—to a monogamous, intimate relationship with our spouse.

God's Design—His Path Leads to Righteous Living

When the Bible says we are created in the image of God, what does that mean? For one, it means that we are created to be in relationship with God. Second, it means we are created for relationships with others. The fact that we serve a God who exists as a Trinity means that he is always in relationship within the Godhead. Only the God of the Bible is relational—no other religion can make that claim. We see this side of God in the first chapter of the Bible: "God said, 'Let us make human beings in our image, to be like us'" (Gen. 1:26). Note that he says "let *us*" and "to be like *us*." Who is the "us"? We believe the "us" refers to the Father, the Son, and the Holy Spirit, each of whom is in relationship with the others. It's really a mystery.

God designed the human person to also be in relationship, and our sexual longings are part of our drive toward that. But the world tries to lure us down its path, whereas God seeks for his children to stay on his path—the ancient path where we live lives of righteousness. Paul, in writing to the Thessalonians, says, "We pleaded with you, encouraged you, and urged you to live your lives in a way that God would consider worthy. For he called you to share in his Kingdom and glory" (1 Thess. 2:12). His words are just as relevant for us today, but they would probably require a stronger plea and more urgent encouragement for us to get the message.

When we were created in God's image, the plan was for us to be like him. But sin entered the picture, Adam and Eve fell by their disobedience, and that has affected every human since. Paul told the Romans, "For everyone has sinned; we all fall short of God's glorious standard" (Rom. 3:23). Not only has every person since Adam and Eve experienced the effects of their disobedience, so have our human cultures. The lies of pornography are evidence of the sinful nature of humankind and of the basic sinfulness of our culture.

One of the first consequences of the fall is the conflict between husband and wife and in many ways between men and women in general. God told Eve, "You will desire to control your husband, but he will rule over you" (Gen. 3:16). This competition between men and women has been compounded in recent generations, in part due to the redefinition of femininity as well as the failed attempt to define what it means to be masculine.

Rather than attempt to understand what the Bible means by submission, our culture has redefined what it means to be a woman—to take charge. And rather than attempt to understand the submissive leadership of men described in the Bible, men often are simply passive. I use the words *submissive leadership* for the husband, based on the introduction to the famous "love your wife" and "submit to your husband" passage, which begins by saying, "Submit to one another out of reverence for Christ" (Eph. 5:21). A man's general passivity is in part responsible for the growth of the pornography industry.

The pattern of passivity in men and the take-charge attitude in women leave a man not really knowing how to relate to a woman. Instead, men talk about how complex a woman is and joke about how impossible it is to really understand her. This all works to keep alive that part of our fallen culture's attempt to continually fuel the competition between the sexes. The result is that many men and women retreat to their preferred pornography—visual images for the men and erotic novels for women.

The problem is compounded for men in that not only do they have limited relationships with women, they have even fewer relationships with other men. In addition, the absence of a father in the home has crippled many men, for they have no image of what healthy manhood really looks like. The result is they live in emotional isolation, which only adds to the seductiveness of all that pornography hidden in their computer. So for a man or a woman to get firmly involved in following God's path requires that we go against the common teachings of our culture.

What's a Man to Do?

So what is a man to do? You may wonder why I don't ask, "What is a man or a woman to do?" Part of my reason is my bias, which is based on how I understand the Bible. When the Bible talks about the man being the head, I think about how our head sets the pace for our lives. Our brain is the source of what we understand, what we perceive, and what we hope to experience. Our brain sets the patterns of our lives. So if we are to understand what the Bible means by the man being the head, then he becomes the one who sets the course for his marriage and for all the relationships in his life. He is not passive. Instead, he is to be a loving initiator.

What the Bible typically calls submission has been given so many different interpretations that I prefer to use a different term. Instead, I say that the wife is basically a responder. She will respond to whatever course the husband will chart. If he is passive, she will take over. If he is a tyrant, she will rebel. If he charts a clear, loving course, she will respond with a sense of feeling secure and loved.

When a husband charts the course in a loving, serving, humble way, he will be walking on God's path. In speaking to married groups and in working with couples in my office, I've found that when I explain this to the husband, the wife agrees. She will typically silently nod her head in agreement along with a knowing smile. I've also found that when a husband becomes a loving initiator, the temptations of those on-screen images are irrelevant to him, for he will have found what God intended. When God created man and woman, he created sex. This man will find true intimacy in his marriage.

So Where Does He Begin?

But how does a man begin to chart a course on God's path? There are several areas in a man's life that need to be involved as he seeks to get back on course or stay on course and set a godly pace in his relationships. How does he restore the broken image of God within? Obviously, since life is basically about relationships, he begins by building relationships. First, the man who is seeking to live a righteous life will always begin by developing relationships with other emotionally healthy men. These are men who have healthy relationships with several other men. A man comes to terms with his issues related to sexual purity in his life in the company of other men. A man learns to be a man through his relationships with other men. The opposite is true as well. A woman learns what it means to be a woman through her relationships with other women.

Notice how this is true developmentally. Watch a playground in an elementary school. Typically, the boys are playing with the boys, and the girls sit and talk with other girls. A boy in the third grade has no interest in girls, nor does a girl at this stage care about boys. This will change, of course, but their exclusive preference to play with others of their own sex is designed by God to prepare them for relationships with the opposite sex as they get older. If we lack some of these same-sex preparatory relationships, we will often end up distorting what God intended in our adult male/female relationships.

This is important also when it comes to our spiritual walk with God, which is the second step a man must take to chart a course on God's path. He needs to become comfortable with his spirituality. Men who are comfortable with other men are usually more comfortable about their relationship with God and, in particular, with Jesus. It takes being comfortable in his masculinity for a man to be in love with Jesus. And he only learns how to be comfortable as a man by building meaningful relationships with other men.

The third aspect that men in particular need to experience is a growing comfort in the world of emotions. Our culture says that men are supposed to be logical and women are supposed to be emotional. Again, this is another way cultural biases keep the competition between men and women alive. A part of being relational for both men and women is to be comfortable in the world of emotions. Real men do cry, and they aren't ashamed to be seen crying.

We were created for relationships, but sin has damaged the image of God within us. Salvation starts a process of restoring and repairing that damaged image. Obviously, we never get to a place where we don't sin, but God has provided a solution for when we do. If you are struggling with guilt and shame over your past, focus on these passages and others you find, and meditate on their confidence that your past has been cleansed—washed clean.

> If we claim we have no sin, we are only fooling ourselves and not living in the truth. But if we confess our sins to him, he is faithful and just to forgive us our sins and to cleanse us from all wickedness. If we claim we have not sinned, we are calling God a liar and showing that his word has no place in our hearts.
>
> My dear children, I am writing this to you so that you will not sin. But if anyone does sin, we have an advocate who pleads our case before the Father. He is Jesus Christ, the one who is truly righteous. He himself is the sacrifice that atones for our sins—and not only our sins but the sins of all the world.[17]

How can I know all the sins lurking in my heart?
Cleanse me from these hidden faults.

Keep your servant from deliberate sins!
 Don't let them control me.
Then I will be free of guilt
 and innocent of great sin.
May the words of my mouth
 and the meditation of my heart
be pleasing to you,
 O LORD, my rock and my redeemer.[18]

Have mercy on me, O God. . . .
Because of your great compassion,
 blot out the stain of my sins.
Wash me clean from my guilt.
 Purify me from my sin. . . .
Purify me from my sins, and I will be clean;
 wash me, and I will be whiter than snow.
Oh, give me back my joy again;
 you have broken me—
 now let me rejoice.
Don't keep looking at my sins.
 Remove the stain of my guilt.
Create in me a clean heart, O God.
 Renew a loyal spirit within me.[19]

Because we have these promises, dear friends, let us cleanse ourselves from everything that can defile our body or spirit. And let us work toward complete holiness because we fear God.[20]

For the grace of God has been revealed, bringing salvation to all people. And we are instructed to turn from godless living and sinful pleasures. We should live in this evil world with wisdom, righteousness, and devotion to God, while we look forward with hope to that wonderful day when the glory of our great God and Savior, Jesus Christ, will be revealed. He gave his life to free us from every kind of sin, to cleanse us, and to make us his very own people, totally committed to doing good deeds.[21]

In addition, when we talk about lust and pornography, we recognize that God's path is a path of purity. Remember what the psalmist asked: "How can a young person [or any person] stay pure? By obeying your word" (Ps. 119:9). Getting the Word of God into our hearts creates and restores the purity of our lives, regardless of our past. Here are some passages that focus on purity:

> Teach me your ways, O LORD,
>   that I may live according to your truth!
> Grant me purity of heart,
>   so that I may honor you.[22]

> Get out! Get out and leave your captivity,
>   where everything you touch is unclean.
> Get out of there and purify yourselves,
>   you who carry home the sacred objects of
>   the LORD.[23]

Humble yourselves before God. Resist the devil, and he will flee from you. Come close to God, and God will come close to you. Wash your hands, you sinners; purify your hearts, for your loyalty is divided between God and the world.[24]

Finally, we choose to make our goal in this life to live a holy lifestyle. People today seem to be more concerned with happiness than with holiness. The purpose in walking God's path is not to attain happiness as if it is a goal. It cannot be a goal, for it is basically what we experience as a result of something else. God's way is to seek first his kingdom, which means we aim for righteous living. His promise is that when we do, we will be fulfilled, and with a sense of fulfillment comes an experience of joy and happiness. Here are a few passages that help us to focus on holy living:

Do not bring shame on my holy name, for I will display my holiness among the people of Israel. I am the LORD who makes you holy.[25]

For by God's grace, I am a special messenger from Christ Jesus to you Gentiles. I bring you the Good News so that I might present you as an acceptable offering to God, made holy by the Holy Spirit.[26]

God has called us to live holy lives, not impure lives.[27]

For the Scriptures say, "You must be holy because I am holy."[28]

In our desire to live righteous lives, it is important to remember that all of our drives—our need for food and water, our need for security, our need for success, and our need for sex—are meant to point us to God. They are all a part of following God's path in this life, not just to prepare us for the next life but to bring us the fulfillment God intended while we live life here on earth his way. Remember what Jeremiah promised to those who choose the godly path: "You will find rest for your souls" (Jer. 6:16).

9

Moving from Modern Idolatry to Contentment

It seems to me that each election cycle shows our country is becoming more and more polarized. Maybe it's always been this way, but in my memory, the last forty years have seen a continuing increase in the hatefulness of character assassinations among politicians. The issues aren't the issues anymore. Instead, we have seen a growing harshness as one candidate attacks his or her opponent solely on the basis of personal character that has nothing to do with the real issues. Now that may have always been a part of politics, but it seems that the politicians have become so polarized that they don't even like each other; in fact, it seems like they hate each other.

The problem goes beyond the politicians. It's affecting the general population as well. I've talked with several people who were afraid to put a bumper sticker on their car this past election, fearing that someone favoring the other candidate would key their car. Others kept their preference secret for fear of getting into a heated argument. It didn't take much awareness to feel the hatred each side seemed to have for the opposition.

We've even added God to the equation. Obviously, God is on *our* side. He agrees with us. We seem to think as author Anne Lamott has said: "You can safely assume you've created God in your own image when it turns out that God hates all the same people you do."[1] Someone else said that when someone hates another person, it appears that idolatry is alive and well in contemporary culture.

Some years ago, I had an interesting conversation with a Messianic Jewish rabbi. In the course of the conversation, he said to me, "You Gentiles don't know how to argue." He went on to point out that in our culture, when one of us gets into a heated argument with someone, we may cut off the other person. They simply stop existing in our world.

Look also at the history of the church. We see the divisions in the Corinthian church, where some wanted to follow Paul, some wanted to follow Apollos, and some wanted to follow Peter, and then there were the believers who insisted they follow only Jesus. There was the division between the Alexandrian believers and the believers in Antioch. There was the split in the church between Rome and the Eastern Church. Another division came when Martin Luther challenged Rome. And think of all the different denominations that have evolved over time. With each division, some group walked away from an argument they weren't able to win.

I remember the old joke where someone in heaven pointed to a group of people all huddled together and asked, "Who are those people over there?" And the answer was, "Oh, they're the _____, and they think they're the only ones here." (You can fill in the blank with the name of any church or denomination.)

My Messianic Jewish friend went on to point out to me that when a group of Jewish people get into an argument, it can get very heated. But when the argument is over, they walk away together, put their arms around each other's shoulders, and go get coffee together.

I have a lithograph in my den of a group of rabbis arguing over the Scriptures. The original was painted by Charles Bragg, and it is titled *Midrash*. In it, five old rabbis are in a very heated discussion, with one pointing at the Scriptures. Every time I look at that picture, I think of my conversation with the Messianic rabbi, and I imagine that when these rabbis are finished with their arguing, they will leave that place arm in arm and go have coffee together. They never made the point of their argument their idol.

Our Typical Definition of Idolatry

If you are like me, you don't think about idolatry very often. Typically, we will think of it when we read something about Israel in the Old Testament. It's easy, then, to assume that all idolatry involves man-made statues that are a part of people's worship. We think also about the first two commandments. The first says, "You must not have any other god but me" (Exod. 20:3). The second commandment goes further and warns, "You must not make for yourself an idol of any kind or an image of anything in the heavens or on the earth or in the sea. You must not bow down to them or worship them, for I, the LORD your God, am a jealous God who will not tolerate your affection for any other gods" (Exod. 20:4–5). So it's easy to think of an idol as some object we make and then worship as a god.

But back to our two paths again. In this chapter, one path has to do with true faith that worships only God; the other is the path of idolatry. God created us to live on the first path. This was his intention in creating us. In Genesis 1:26–28, God said,

> "Let us make human beings in our image, to be like us. They will reign over the fish in the sea, the birds in the sky, the livestock, all the wild animals on the earth, and the small animals that scurry along the ground."

> So God created human beings in his own image.
> In the image of God he created them;
> male and female he created them.

> Then God blessed them and said, "Be fruitful and multiply. Fill the earth and govern it. Reign over the fish in the sea, the birds in the sky, and all the animals that scurry along the ground."

Humans were created to worship God and to rule over all of creation. But then in the third chapter of Genesis,

Adam and Eve sinned. They purposely disobeyed God. As a result, they were evicted from the Garden of Eden, and all of life changed for them. And it changed for us as well. The apostle Paul understood the result of their disobedience, as Adam and Eve had chosen the path of idolatry. Paul wrote about people in general,

> They knew God, but they wouldn't worship him as God or even give him thanks. And they began to think up foolish ideas of what God was like. As a result, their minds became dark and confused. Claiming to be wise, they instead became utter fools. And instead of worshiping the glorious, ever-living God, they worshiped idols made to look like mere people and birds and animals and reptiles. . . .
>
> They traded the truth about God for a lie. So they worshiped and served the things God created instead of the Creator himself, who is worthy of eternal praise! Amen. (Rom. 1:21–23, 25)

What God intended was for humans to worship him and then to use all of creation for their benefit. What Paul is saying is that we have reversed the order. We try to use God for our own benefit as we worship and serve created things. The reality is that eventually these created things will begin to rule our lives. The created order God intended in Genesis 1 has been reversed.

One of the results of that reversal is that when we are on the path of idolatry, our souls are never content. We are always searching for more, thinking it will bring contentment. But Solomon warned us when he wrote, "Everything is wearisome beyond description. No matter how much we see, we are never satisfied. No matter how much we hear, we are not content" (Eccles. 1:8).

What Solomon and Paul are saying is that either we worship and serve God, or we worship and serve what we create as our idols. Since I don't have any statues that I worship, what do I do that can be called idolatry?

What do you worship?

Modern Forms of Idolatry

Our modern definition of idolatry goes beyond images and statues. It has to do with the desires of the heart. Where do I focus my energy? What has captured my imagination and my heart? On what I am building my life? What is it that drives me? To make an idol out of something today means we are giving it love, attention, and energy with nothing much left for God.

Foundational to all modern forms of idolatry is the worship of "me." Its focus is on what I want. Anything I have become addicted to becomes an idol.

Take the person addicted to a drug. Their addiction forces them to be thinking constantly about where they are going to get their next fix. The big problem today is the addiction to prescription drugs, to pain relievers. Think about how much time and energy the addicted person focuses on getting the necessary prescriptions and not letting one doctor know about the other doctor. Maybe the addiction has progressed to the point where the doctors' prescriptions need to be supplemented by what can be bought on the streets. Eventually, there's no time for much else, and God is only in the picture when the person is in trouble and desperately needs help. The pills, or drug of choice, have become an idol.

Let's take a milder example. What about our work and our need to make money? How many hours a week do we put into our efforts to "get ahead" financially? Some people will spend twelve hours a day, seven days a week. How much more money do we need? I talked with a man who set a goal as a boy that by the time he was forty he would be a millionaire. He made his goal, but in the process he lost his wife, and to this day his kids won't speak to him. Money was his idol.

Money is probably the most popular idol today. But it also was in Jesus's day. In Matthew, Jesus is quoted as saying, "No one can serve two masters. For you will hate one and love the other; you will be devoted to one and despise the other. You cannot serve both God and money" (Matt. 6:24). The one you serve will be the one you worship.

In his parable of the sower, Jesus states, "The seed that fell among the thorns represents others who hear God's word, but all too quickly the message is crowded out by the worries of this life, the lure of wealth, and the desire for other things, so no fruit is produced" (Mark 4:18–19). Again, Jesus presents a choice: hear the Word and worship God and produce fruit, or focus on worries, wealth, and desires, with the result of ending up with nothing. One could accurately say that the focus of our worries represents the idols in our lives.

What about sports? If idolatry is defined as God hating who you hate, you don't have to go too far to find some fanatically obsessed sports fans. Their life revolves around their teams, one for each sport and season of the year. Look at what happens when a team that isn't "your team" loses the championship. There are riots in the streets of that city. Talk about anger and hatred.

Now I know not every sports fan hits the idolatry quotient. But we can add to the mix the obsession our culture has with sports personalities or with other celebrities. I watched a television interview segment whose hosts stopped people randomly and showed them pictures of celebrities. Every person questioned, regardless of their age, could identify every one of the celebrities. But when shown pictures of political leaders or famous historical figures, very few could identify them. Idolatry takes place when we go beyond being fans to following every detail of the celebrities' lives.

We could include pop musicians and bands. And what about automobiles? Or NASCAR? All of these have the potential for becoming an idol. In fact, whatever controls our time and attention becomes our god. If our life is controlled by a search for power, for acceptance, for fame, for vicariously enjoying the victory of our team, then we are living in a fantasy of being in control. In truth, we are controlled by the gods of our lives.

Someone from another culture where shrines and altars are prevalent was commenting on her perception of America's idols. She said we obviously worship food, for that was clear from all the restaurants we have. Then she suggested another one of our idols was sports, and she based that on the "shrines" we have built for our sports teams. She was, of course, referring to the stadiums. And then she said one of our most popular idols had to be our televisions, for everybody's family room is arranged to give homage to the television. I'm sure there are many more idols in our culture.

Here are some passages to meditate on. As you do, relate your meditation to the modern definition of idolatry. Or if you can identify your personal idols, think about them as you meditate.

Even when you ask, you don't get it because your motives are all wrong—you want only what will give you pleasure.

You adulterers! Don't you realize that friendship with the world makes you an enemy of God? I say it again: If you want to be a friend of the world, you make yourself an enemy of God. What do you think the Scriptures mean when they say that the spirit God has placed within us is filled with envy [meaning God wants us for himself]?[2]

Put to death the sinful, earthly things lurking within you. Have nothing to do with sexual immorality, impurity, lust, and evil desires. Don't be greedy, for a greedy person is an idolater, worshiping the things of this world. Because of these sins, the anger of God is coming.[3]

Then when they are exiled among the nations, they will remember me. They will recognize how hurt I am by their unfaithful hearts and lustful eyes that long for their idols. Then at last they will hate themselves for all their detestable sins. They will know that I alone am the LORD and that I was serious when I said I would bring this calamity on them.[4]

> Rebellion is as sinful as witchcraft,
>> and stubbornness as bad as worshiping idols.[5]

> Those who worship false gods
>> turn their backs on all God's mercies.[6]

And what union can there be between God's temple and idols? For we are the temple of the living God. As God said:

> I will live in them
>> and walk among them.
> I will be their God,
>> and they will be my people.[7]

There is an interesting event that occurred in the city of Ephesus when Paul was ministering there. For two years Paul lectured daily in that city. What an experience that must have been! In addition, God worked unusual miracles where people were healed simply by touching something Paul had worn. Even the demons got involved when they challenged seven priests who were trying to cast them out of a person using Jesus's name. One demon said, "I know Jesus, and I know Paul, but who are you?" (Acts 19:15), and then it brutally attacked the seven priests. All of this had a great impact on the people of that city.

But the powerful effect of Paul's ministry in Ephesus went too far for some of the local businessmen. One businessman in particular, Demetrius, made silver images of the goddess Diana, or Artemis. Artemis was the local goddess who was the object of worship in Ephesus. Demetrius was obviously concerned about the impact on his business if people left the worship of Artemis and turned to Jesus.

After sharing his concern with other local businessmen, Demetrius turned to the people and called on them to defend their goddess. They wouldn't riot over his loss of income, and he knew that, but they would riot to protect their goddess, who was being threatened by the number of people becoming Christians. But the riot that followed was not started because the businessmen wanted to defend their goddess, although they used that theme to rile the people. Demetrius started the protest because the number of people who were choosing to follow God's path were hurting their business. Their wealth—their true idol—was at stake. They claimed allegiance to Artemis, but their real god was their money. It was only the mayor's fear of the Roman reaction to the riot, and his letting the people know this concern, that he was able to restore calmness. (See the account in Acts 19.)

The account is an interesting picture of how we can hide our real idols behind paying lip service to the correct "god." But eventually, our behavior will reveal our true object of worship. Martin Luther said that whatever our heart clings to and confides in is really our god. It doesn't matter what we say, our life demonstrates our allegiance to our god.

So What's the Alternative?

If idolatry represents a restlessness that results from our seeking to control our lives, then God's path is based on our allowing him to control our lives. "His will, not ours" is more than a motto, it is how we are to choose to live. To live any other way is to take away from God what is rightfully his. All things we have and enjoy come from his hand. They are not to be taken as "mine." They are his gifts to us. This is really the key to breaking free from our idols and learning to live a life of contentment.

We experience a life of contentment as we walk on the godly path, worshiping the Creator and enjoying his creation. Contentment is a state of the mind. It is a calm and satisfied feeling that is free from complaints. But it is not a natural state of mind. Our natural response to unpleasant circumstances is to covet someone else's good fortune or to murmur and complain. Over time, these states of mind can become dominated by bitterness and resentment. These are as natural to humans as are the weeds or thorns that grow naturally in the soil. But we have to cultivate the experience of contentment. Contentment does not happen on its own.

Paul was a contented man. In writing to the Philippians, he said, "I have learned how to be content with whatever I have. I know how to live on almost nothing or with everything. I have learned the secret of living in every situation, whether it is with a full stomach or empty, with plenty or little. For I can do everything through Christ, who gives me strength" (Phil. 4:11–13). Paul had learned to be content in all circumstances because Christ strengthened him in every circumstance. That's why he could say in Philippians 1:21, "For to me, to live is Christ" (NIV).

In addition, Paul wrote to his protégé Timothy and said, "True godliness with contentment is itself great wealth" (1 Tim. 6:6). Paul is saying that true wealth is having a godly character, and when we develop that, we experience the happiness that comes with contentment. In other words, he couples godliness with a state of contentment. They go together! When we are consciously developing our relationship with God and with Jesus Christ, that is also true godliness.

There are several things we can learn from Paul. First, as I said earlier, contentment doesn't come naturally. We all suffer from the effects of Adam and Eve's disobedience. That means our natural behavior is to move from honoring and worshiping the Creator to worshiping created things. That was Paul's natural experience before he *learned* to be content in all situations. It is our natural experience as well.

Second, note the extremes of Paul's circumstances. He knew how to live on almost nothing. Are you able to say you are happy and content when someone else gets the promotion you expected? Or how does it feel when someone takes the credit for the work you did? The King James Version uses the word *abased* in Philippians 4:12. That's a kind of contentment we have to learn. It doesn't come naturally to any of us.

Maybe it's easier for those who have never had much. I talked with someone who ministers frequently in the Dominican Republic, and she told me how she loves the little church she and her husband attend when they are there. She explained that the people in that church live in abject poverty, but they are the happiest and most contented people she has ever met. That's not an uncommon experience.

The opposite, I believe, is much more difficult. I've found that the more things people have and the more money they have, the more discontented they are with their life. How do people handle success? Those still striving for it believe that once they get there, they will be content. But my experience in working with successful people is that few of them really are happy and content. In fact, those who are very successful financially are always on edge, worrying about what might happen to their money.

Finally, Paul experienced both having wealth and having nothing, and he learned in both situations how to be content. The important thing to note is *learning* how. The question is how did he learn to be content? How did he break the natural cycle we all struggle with? There is nothing to be learned simply in not having enough or in having too much, in being hungry or in being satisfied. It takes something or someone beyond us to help us learn contentment.

Obviously, Paul discovered how to be content by shifting from the worship of material things and people to the worship and centrality of God the Creator. Food, money, fame—none of these were his focus. His focus was solely on worshiping and pleasing Christ.

It's important to note that this is the context for the oft-quoted words in Philippians 4:13 where Paul says, "For I can do everything through Christ, who gives me strength." How often do we claim that verse as a promise that we can do some great task? But notice the context. Paul is giving us the answer to how we can be content in this life. It's like he is saying, "I have learned to be content in spite of my circumstances because my relationship with Christ is central to my life. Jesus Christ is the key to my contentment!" For Paul, there was only one thing to worship in his life. That was the person of Jesus Christ. He wrote earlier in his letter to the Philippians, "For to me, living means living for Christ" (1:21).

My pastor preached a series of sermons asking whether we were fans or followers of Jesus. Idolatry could be defined as not being willing to cross the line from being simply a fan to actually becoming a follower of Jesus Christ and walking on the godly path.

I think we probably begin our walk with Jesus by being fans. After all, he is the one who provided for our salvation. But if we stay just a fan, we haven't captured what Paul meant by "living for Christ." The consequence of being only a fan is that we are vulnerable to a multitude of idols that we may choose to worship. Look at the difference when we actually become a follower of Jesus. We make him our priority, we expend our energy to grow in our relationship with him, and we seek to obey him as we follow him daily. When we do this, we will experience the contentment that comes from walking on the godly path.

The question is "What or whom are you following?" Whatever we are followers of can become our own personal idols. Jesus put it this way: "Wherever your treasure is, there the desires of your heart will also be" (Luke 12:34). To help you focus on what it means to live for Christ, spend some time meditating on the following passages.

I am making this covenant with you so that no one among you—no man, woman, clan, or tribe—will turn away from the Lord our God to worship these gods of other nations, and so that no root among you bears bitter and poisonous fruit.[8]

> Don't wear yourself out trying to get rich.
>   Be wise enough to know when to quit.
> In the blink of an eye wealth disappears,
>   for it will sprout wings
>   and fly away like an eagle.[9]

Those who love money will never have enough. How meaningless to think that wealth brings true happiness! The more you have, the more people come to help you spend it. So what good is wealth—except perhaps to watch it slip through your fingers![10]

Your Father knows exactly what you need even before you ask him![11]

Don't worry about these things, saying, "What will we eat? What will we drink? What will we wear?" These things dominate the thoughts of unbelievers, but your heavenly Father already knows all your needs. Seek the Kingdom of God above all else, and live righteously, and he will give you everything you need.

So don't worry about tomorrow, for tomorrow will bring its own worries. Today's trouble is enough for today.[12]

You cannot become my disciple without giving up everything you own.[13]

My dear friends, flee from the worship of idols.[14]

Their god is their appetite, they brag about shameful things, and they think only about this life here on earth. But we are citizens of heaven, where the Lord Jesus Christ lives. And we are eagerly waiting for him to return as our Savior.[15]

Don't worry about anything; instead, pray about everything. Tell God what you need, and thank him for all he has done. Then you will experience God's peace, which exceeds anything we can understand. His peace will guard your hearts and minds as you live in Christ Jesus.[16]

True godliness with contentment is itself great wealth.[17]

So if we have enough food and clothing, let us be content.

But people who long to be rich fall into temptation and are trapped by many foolish and harmful desires that plunge them into ruin and destruction. For the love of money is the root of all kinds of evil. And some people, craving money, have wandered from the true faith and pierced themselves with many sorrows.

But you, Timothy, are a man of God; so run from all these evil things. Pursue righteousness and a godly life, along with faith, love, perseverance, and gentleness.[18]

Don't love money; be satisfied with what you have. For God has said,

> "I will never fail you.
> I will never abandon you."[19]

Give all your worries and cares to God, for he cares about you.[20]

Dear children, keep away from anything that might take God's place in your hearts.[21]

For centuries, the Jewish people had an affirmation that they repeated. It was "We have no king but God!" Then, during the time of Samuel, the people didn't like Samuel's sons. They were corrupt and the people didn't want them to be judges, so the Israelites banded together and demanded that they have a king. They wanted to be like the other nations around them.

Reluctantly, Samuel conferred with God, and God said, "Give them a king." But the affirmation continued— "We have no king but God!" Then it grew weaker, only to resurface when the Jewish people were in exile, and even after they returned to Jerusalem. But it didn't have the same meaning to the people. And the loss of meaning in that affirmation was tragically true of the religious leaders.

With that background, look at what happened in the trial of Jesus before Pilate, as reported by John:

Pilate said to the people, "Look, here is your king!"

"Away with him," they yelled. "Away with him! Crucify him!"

"What? Crucify your king?" Pilate asked.

"We have no king but Caesar," the leading priests shouted back.

Then Pilate turned Jesus over to them to be crucified. (John 19:14–16)

What had happened to "We have no king but God"? Even the religious leaders had forgotten its significance. What was left was idolatry and discontent.

What about us? The question of idolatry is really "Who is your king?" The answer of the contented man or woman is "I have no king but Jesus!" When we make anything else king in our lives, we lose any chance at contentment. When we have no king but Jesus, we've found the true source of contentment.

10

Moving from Life's Trials to Joy

The book of James begins with a hard statement. James writes, "Dear brothers and sisters, when troubles come your way, consider it an opportunity for great joy" (1:2). How do we do that? Do we celebrate our troubles? Do we seek troubles? I don't believe that's what he is saying. But the juxtaposition of troubles and joy has led to some strange ideas.

The difficulty with this passage is compounded by the fact that when many of us are suffering or are struggling with some kind of trouble, our first reaction is to ask, "Where is God?" Then the other common question follows: "Why is this happening to me?"

Harold is a good example of this. Harold is a Realtor, and for several years there were a lot of Realtors who couldn't make a living selling houses, so they left the field. Sales were sparse, and competition between Realtors was high. Harold was committed to staying on the job, even though he hadn't had a deal in over a year. His reserves were almost all gone, and at one point in our conversation, he said he was about a month away from being homeless.

He was angry, of course. And a lot of his anger was directed at God: "Why doesn't God help me?" "Where is God?" "I work hard. Why hasn't he done his part?" "I don't even know why I keep thinking God's even interested in me." "Is God punishing me?" "Is God telling me to get out of real estate and do something else? But I love what I'm doing. Why would God want that of me?" These were only some of his questions. At this point, he had stopped going to church, had stopped going to any Bible studies, and, out of embarrassment, had cut off his relationships with almost all of his friends. He was increasingly alone in his suffering.

How do these words from James—"when troubles come your way, consider it an opportunity for great joy"—help Harold? It doesn't matter what translation someone might use to quote that verse to him, it would only add to his anger and cynicism. But I did quote it, along with some others. And I listened to his bitter responses. Yet I kept him talking about the character of God: how he doesn't desert us in the midst of troubles and how he has something for us to learn through difficult times.

I talked to him about the Israelites living in captivity for over four hundred years. They worked as slaves, and thanks to Moses's efforts to do God's bidding, their work became even more unbearable. Some gave up on God, some questioned God, others continued to trust God. Even after God delivered them, they ended up wandering in the desert for forty years. During that time, they complained and even wanted to go back to Egypt and to their enslavement. They all went through the same troubles, but some trusted while others continued to complain.

Then we talked about the biblical character Job. Isn't it interesting that so many of us think the book of Job gives us an explanation about suffering and life's trials? I still haven't found an answer to why people suffer anywhere in that book. Yes, we are told that his troubles came because God and Satan were having a conversation about him in heaven one day. But that doesn't help me understand why there are suffering and troubles in this life.

But here's what I do understand about Job, and what I explained to Harold. Job argued with God for more than thirty chapters, and God never rebuked him for arguing. In addition, much to our distress, it appears that God never really told Job what went on in the conversation between him and Satan. I've always thought that a better ending to the book would have been for God to put his arm around Job and say, "Here's what took place one day in heaven. I'm sorry." But that's not what happened. What God did do in the last chapters of the book was to deeply challenge Job and expand his understanding of who God really is. And when Job understood that, he repented.

What had Job done that required repentance? It wasn't his arguing, for the Jewish tradition still sees arguing with God as a form of prayer. Job wasn't the only one to argue with God; so did Abraham in Genesis 18. Abraham kept arguing for fewer believers in Sodom and Gomorrah, to change God's decision to destroy the cities.

The only thing I can find that Job needed to repent about was his limited understanding of who God is—his character and his nature. He had God in a box, and God exploded the box with his series of questions—many of which still can't be answered.

So how did this relate to Harold? Like what happens to so many of us, when he ran into life's troubles, his understanding of God shrank. We think that God's primary purpose in our life is to protect us from troubles. But then we encounter passages like James 1:3, which says, "You know that when your faith is tested, your endurance has a chance to grow," or Romans 5, where Paul says the same thing: "We can rejoice, too, when we run into problems and trials, for we know that they help us develop endurance. And endurance develops strength of character, and character strengthens our confident hope of salvation. And this hope will not lead to disappointment. For we know how dearly God loves us" (vv. 3–5). Both James and Paul are saying that life's trials have a purpose—to produce endurance and strengthen our faith. But in the midst of our trial, we're usually not interested in learning more endurance.

But back to Harold. I asked him to meditate on the ending chapter of Job, where Job replied to God the second time by saying,

> I know that you can do anything,
>   and no one can stop you.
> You asked, "Who is this that questions my wis-
>   dom with such ignorance?"

It is I—and I was talking about things I knew
    nothing about,
things far too wonderful for me.
You said, "Listen and I will speak!
    I have some questions for you,
    and you must answer them."
I had only heard about you before,
    but now I have seen you with my own eyes.
I take back everything I said,
    and I sit in dust and ashes to show my
        repentance.

Job 42:2–6

Job surrendered to a God who was bigger than his questions!

We Don't Like Trouble

When life's trials hit us, our first instinct is to fight back. We don't think of surrendering. That would be defeat. No one likes it when faced with the pain and suffering that come with life's troubles. That's because we don't like to experience pain. That's a universal that crosses all cultural barriers.

The pain of our trials is so very personal. I remember a conversation with a friend who was very frustrated with the length of his son's hair. This was back when long hair was still seen as a negative or rebellious behavior. At the same time, we had been going through some intense issues with one of our own kids. As he talked, he suddenly stopped and said,

199

"I don't have any right to complain. What's upsetting me is so minor compared to what you've been through." I pointed out to him that he did have a right to complain, because his pain was personal and wasn't to be compared with anyone else's. Whatever your life's trouble is about, the pain you feel is your pain, and only you know its intensity.

What Happens in Our Brain

When we are hit by one of life's trials, what happens when we are confronted with a problem over which we have little or no control? What goes on in our brain? The reaction in our brain is similar to what happens when we experience a lot of stress. Harold's stress level was off the charts. He had already lost his house through foreclosure, and he was a month behind in his rent. In addition, his payments on his car were already two months behind. He lived in fear that if he were evicted from his home, he couldn't even live in his car—it would be repossessed. The next question he raised was how he could continue to work without a car.

Harold's amygdala was working overtime warning his hippocampus that trouble was here. The pituitary gland was busy signaling the release of cortisol and the other stress hormones. Remember, these hormones are released to prepare us for action—to either fight or take flight. But Harold was frozen by his fear of what was just around the corner. He wanted to run, but there was no place to go to get away from his troubles. And he was too depressed to really succeed in his work. He was convinced he was a long way from being able to rejoice in his situation.

Typically, the world's way of dealing with this kind of hopeless situation is to self-medicate. Alcohol will stimulate the pleasure center in the brain for a short time and give some superficial relief. But Harold was a recovering alcoholic, and at this point that was out of the question. He wondered if he should visit his doctor and ask for a prescription for something to help him cope. But that could be just as dangerous as drinking.

Life's Trials Do Have a Purpose

It's easy to say, "Yes, I know we live in a sinful world and bad things happen to good people. But why me?" To understand life's trials, we need to get beyond the "why me?" question and begin to look seriously at God's words on the reason we experience these trials. There is a purpose to them. But we often don't look for the purpose, because one of our first responses is to think we are being punished by God. Once we put our trials into that context, it is hard to change our thinking.

Our painful trials hurt too much, and because they hurt, we feel like we are being punished. I've talked to people who are leery of a relationship with God. They refer to Hebrews 12:5–6, which says, "My child, don't make light of the LORD's discipline, and don't give up when he corrects you. For the LORD disciplines those he loves, and he punishes each one he accepts as his child." Who wants a relationship with a God who punishes his followers?

Now, we could say that this passage is referring to punishment, and part of it does. But why and when does God "punish"? Think first of why parents punish their child. It's not because the parents are mean, it's because the child needs correction. When my child does something wrong, I correct him, and that may involve punishment. He may be grounded for a week, or he may not be able to drive for a week—something like that would be a punishment that is designed to correct wrong behavior.

For example, if I have spent myself into a corner so that I can't pay my bills, does God's silence in response to my cry for help mean he is punishing me? Probably. But the purpose of his punishment is to correct my wrong behavior. Someone has said to me that it is foolish to try to pray our way out of something we behaved our way into. So God's silence to Harold may have to do with correcting some pattern of behavior in his life that doesn't please God. He needs to examine himself on that issue.

But all of life's problems are not intended to correct wrong behavior. Therefore, they are not in the category of punishment. The apostle Paul gives us a different context for understanding another of God's purposes in relation to our trials—the realm of athletics. An athlete who is preparing to compete in the Olympics, or on any level, will train for that competition. If the sport is running, the athlete will run, lift weights, and in other ways work at strengthening himself or herself in order to be competitive. The training program will undoubtedly cause the athlete to experience pain. The saying is "no pain, no gain." This is true in any sport—training for excellence is going to involve pain. So Paul wrote in 1 Corinthians 9:25–27, "All athletes are disciplined in their training. They do it to win a prize that will fade away, but we do it for an eternal prize. So I run with purpose in every step. I am not just shadowboxing. I discipline my body like an athlete, training it to do what it should."

Life's trials can be a part of the discipline we need in order to experience all that God wants for us. They train our soul to do what God designed it to do. If we take the imagery that Paul is using and put our life's trial into that context, we can begin to see that God's purpose in allowing that particular trial might be positive. It may be that we need to purify our life or mature in our faith in some way. Or maybe there is something else God wants us to learn through the situation.

Hebrews tells us, "It was only right that he [God] should make Jesus, through his suffering, a perfect leader" (2:10). And again we read, "Even though Jesus was God's Son, he learned obedience from the things he suffered" (5:8). We are to follow Jesus's example. We also learn obedience from the things we suffer, if we allow God to be God and know that he wants only the best for us in all circumstances.

Is My Trial from God?

How can we discern what is the cause of a painful situation? How was Harold going to find God's purpose in his situation? If it is God's discipline in the sense of a parent disciplining a child, then it is obviously from God. It is the result of something in my life that I need to correct, some area of disobedience. I can tell that it is discipline because there will be a relationship between the discipline and the disobedience. My response needs to be a rejection of the "why?" question and instead be, "What do I need to learn about myself in this situation? What do I need to change?" When this happens, I can rejoice, for God is saying to me that I am his beloved child.

If my trial does not fit the description above of God's discipline, then I can consider it a testing of my faith. My trial may simply be due to my living in a sinful world, or it may be brought on directly as an attack by Satan. It is also happening because I am seeking to be a follower, not just a fan, as stated in the previous chapter. I can discern which is true by asking if the trial is a test of my faith, my commitment to follow Jesus. If my answer is yes, then my response is to persevere, or as both Paul and James said, to learn endurance. And there is joy in this, for there is always a reward. James tells us that "God blesses those who patiently endure testing and temptation. Afterward they will receive the crown of life that God has promised to those who love him" (1:12).

Take some time now and meditate on these passages that will help you understand God's purpose in the trials of your life:

> "Don't be afraid," Moses answered them, "for God has come in this way to test you, and so that your fear of him will keep you from sinning!"[1]

Remember how the LORD your God led you through the wilderness for these forty years, humbling you and testing you to prove your character, and to find out whether or not you would obey his commands. Yes, he humbled you by letting you go hungry and then feeding you with manna, a food previously unknown to you and your ancestors. He did it to teach you that people do not live by bread alone; rather, we live by every word that comes from the mouth of the LORD.[2]

> Let the whole world bless our God
>> and loudly sing his praises.
> Our lives are in his hands,
>> and he keeps our feet from stumbling.
> You have tested us, O God;
>> you have purified us like silver.
> You captured us in your net
>> and laid the burden of slavery on our backs.
> Then you put a leader over us.
>> We went through fire and flood,
>> but you brought us to a place of great
>> abundance.[3]

That is why we never give up. Though our bodies are dying, our spirits are being renewed every day. For our present troubles are small and won't last very long. Yet they produce for us a glory that vastly outweighs them and will last forever! So we don't look at the troubles we can see now; rather, we fix our gaze on things that cannot be seen. For the things we see now will soon be gone, but the things we cannot see will last forever.[4]

I am glad when I suffer for you in my body, for I am participating in the sufferings of Christ that continue for his body, the church.[5]

Everyone who wants to live a godly life in Christ Jesus will suffer persecution.[6]

Do not throw away this confident trust in the Lord. Remember the great reward it brings you! Patient endurance is what you need now, so that you will continue to do God's will. Then you will receive all that he has promised.[7]

When troubles come your way, consider it an opportunity for great joy. For you know that when your faith is tested, your endurance has a chance to grow. So let it grow, for when your endurance is fully developed, you will be perfect and complete, needing nothing.[8]

So be truly glad. There is wonderful joy ahead, even though you have to endure many trials for a little while. These trials will show that your faith is genuine. It is being tested as fire tests and purifies gold—though your faith is far more precious than mere gold. So when your faith remains strong through many trials, it will bring you much praise and glory and honor on the day when Jesus Christ is revealed to the whole world.[9]

For God is pleased with you when you do what you know is right and patiently endure unfair treatment. Of course, you get no credit for being patient if you are beaten for doing wrong. But if you suffer for doing good and endure it patiently, God is pleased with you.

For God called you to do good, even if it means suffering, just as Christ suffered for you.[10]

Since Christ suffered physical pain, you must arm yourselves with the same attitude he had, and be ready to suffer, too. For if you have suffered physically for Christ, you have finished with sin. You won't spend the rest of your lives chasing your own desires, but you will be anxious to do the will of God.[11]

When we walk on God's path, we will experience joy. It's like a friend of mine who, whenever a trial comes along, says, "Oh good. God is going to teach me something new!" That's what joy in the midst of the circumstances is all about.

What Happens in Our Brain When We Experience Joy

Central to our brain's experience of joy is the hypothalamus. In addition, other parts of the limbic system are activated, especially the nucleus accumbens. This small cluster of cells in the limbic system, located in the forebrain, is well connected to the amygdala. The nucleus accumbens is also connected to other parts of the emotional center of our brain. In the context of joy, the primary task of this small part of the brain is to store up the neurotransmitter substance called dopamine. When we experience joy, dopamine is released into the limbic system.

It's interesting that when we take a pain medication or use an opioid, cocaine, or an amphetamine, the nucleus accumbens does the same thing as when we experience joy: it releases dopamine into the limbic system. But as opposed to what happens when we experience joy, these substitutes eventually work against themselves. Over time, increased dosages are required to achieve the same effect. And that leads to addiction.

God designed our brain for us to experience joy the natural way. He knew that our pain could be regulated by our attitude, in particular the expressions of joy and love. The question is how can we reach the place of joy without the use of pain pills, alcohol, or illegal drugs? Harold found the answer, and it started with meditating on Scripture and then taking action, which for him was a dramatic step.

The Power of Surrender

Harold used to turn to alcohol when he experienced stress and soon found that he couldn't control his drinking. He was an alcoholic. He started attending AA, stopped his drinking, and got into recovery. One of the twelve steps of AA is to surrender, but for Harold, surrendering anything beyond his drinking had always escaped his understanding. But as he reflected on the final chapter of the book of Job, he finally understood. Here's what he shared with me.

When he experienced this understanding of the meaning of surrender, he realized it meant surrendering everything to God. Not just his drinking but every detail of his life. So he literally got on the floor facedown, spread out his arms, opened his hands, and prayed. In his prayer, he gave every facet of his predicament to God. He said to God, "Now it's your problem!" By that he meant that even if he couldn't pay his rent, couldn't pay his car payment, and didn't have any money for food, he still was surrendering all of it to God. And he surrendered every other aspect of his life he could think of. He said he must have been on the floor like that for almost an hour.

This wasn't just a onetime act. And it didn't mean he would sit and wait for God to act—he gave the problems to God and went to work confident that God was in control. Each morning he went through the same process (except not on the floor).

Harold went on to say that if he started to stress about his rent, he again would pray and surrender that problem to God. Gradually things started to change. He got a call from a former client who wanted him to sell their house. Then someone he had recently met, who was interested in buying a house, called him out of the blue. He hadn't talked with that person for over a month. Business started to happen for him. He was able to borrow some money against his commission in order to pay his rent. Whenever the old doubts would resurface, he would stop and pray, consciously surrendering the problem to God once again.

As we talked about the change, I noted that one of the things I saw in him was a new confidence. Instead of fighting off the feelings of depression as he recited all his fears, he was now open and positive. I said to him that he now had an inviting spirit that seemed to draw people to him, whereas before he was so down no one wanted to spend much time with him. In that state of mind, I don't think anyone would have wanted to work with him.

As I write this, Harold hasn't resolved all of his life's problems, but he is on the right path, and he is experiencing joy for the first time in a long time.

An unknown Confederate soldier wrote a poem titled "A Creed for Those Who Have Suffered." It describes the way God often works in our lives, especially in terms of our trials and tests.

> I asked God for strength, that I might achieve.
> I was made weak, that I might learn humbly to obey.
> I asked for health, that I might do great things.
> I was given infirmity, that I might do better things.
> I asked for riches, that I might be happy.
> I was given poverty, that I might be wise.
> I asked for power, that I might have the praise of men.
> I was given weakness, that I might feel the need of God.
> I asked for all things, that I might enjoy life.
> I was given life, that I might enjoy all things.
> I got nothing I asked for—but everything I had hoped for.
> Almost despite myself, my unspoken prayers were answered.
> I am, among men, most richly blessed.

This soldier's unspoken prayers came from a surrendered heart. It's interesting how God works. He is so illogical. Jesus said, "If you try to hang on to your life, you will lose it. But if you give up your life for my sake, you will save it" (Luke 9:24). If you want to rejoice when life's trials come your way, surrender yourself to God. That doesn't mean you sit and wait. You don't stop; you just keep on keeping on with a surrendered heart. If you want to enjoy life and experience joy, then learn how to daily surrender everything in your life—both the good and the bad. Instead of asking "why?" or "why me?" ask the question of God, "What do you need for me to learn in this experience?" That is a world changer and a mind renewer.

Afterword

This is not just a book to read; it is meant to be experienced. You can start slowly, but until you allow yourself to spend at least thirty minutes four times a week on this journey, you will miss out on how incredible God's plan is for helping you to rethink how you think. Real change is possible, but it requires—and here's that word we love to avoid—discipline. We have to be serious about transformation. It can't be a hit-or-miss program. The psalmist said that he delighted "in the law [Word] of the LORD, meditating on it day and night" (Ps. 1:2). He was serious about transformation in his life.

After you have spent some time meditating on the passages listed in the previous six chapters, you may want to continue by meditating on one of Paul's letters, such as Galatians. Or you may want to meditate on one of the Gospels. Continue the process wherever you choose. You can use a translation you are familiar with, or you may want to use a different translation so it is fresh for you—either way, the benefit is in the doing, and in staying with the process. Take a few verses at a time or focus in on a paragraph or two. I use the New Living Translation and often focus on a section of several paragraphs set apart in the text by a title. It's important not to try to cover too much at a time. But it's up to you to gauge how much you want to bite off at once.

As you practice discursive meditation, you will find that your questions about the Scriptures and about doctrines become secondary to simply allowing the Scriptures to speak directly to your heart. God's Word is living, and the apostle John makes that clear in his introduction to his Gospel. He wrote, "In the beginning the Word already existed. The Word was with God, and the Word was God" (John 1:1). It doesn't get any clearer than that—Jesus is the Word. They are one and the same. When you truly encounter the Scriptures, you are encountering who Jesus is—the living God!

As you meditate on or prayerfully memorize the Scriptures, you are planting God's Word deep within the center of your being so that it can live out its reality in your life. This is really the only way the Bible can become formative in how you live. You are actually allowing the Word to become flesh (see John 1:14).

The writer of Hebrews also urges us to "stop going over the basic teachings about Christ again and again. Let us go on instead and become mature in our understanding" (6:1). As you faithfully allow God's Word to penetrate the center of your being, you will experience a maturing process in your relationship with Jesus.

Writer and pastor Eugene Peterson commented on Jesus's encounter with the religious teacher who asked what he needed to do to inherit eternal life. As Luke records this story for us, he lets us see that the question had a hostile intent. The religious teacher is testing Jesus. Jesus responds with an interesting question. He asks, "What does the law of Moses say? How do you read it?" (Luke 10:26). The expert in religious law of course knows the answer—he knows the law. But Jesus also asks him, "How do you read it?"

When he gives the correct factual answer, Jesus simply tells him to go and do what Moses said he should do. But the religious teacher isn't satisfied. He had failed in his attempt to trap Jesus, so he asks another question, this one more complex: "And who is my neighbor?" (v. 29). Jesus answers with the story of the good Samaritan. (See Luke 10:25–37.)

The teacher of religion knew the words, he knew the definitions, he even knew the doctrines. But he ignored Jesus's question about how he read the law of Moses. What Jesus was asking him was, "Do you read the Scriptures just for the knowledge you can accumulate, or do you read them in a way that allows them to change your life?" Jesus affirmed that the man knew his material but pressed him to see if he had ever allowed the teaching to touch his life. The point of Jesus's story about the good Samaritan was to confront the scholar with the need not only to accumulate knowledge but to live out the meaning of the Scriptures genuinely.

Discursive meditation on Scripture confronts us with the living Word, which works to change us into what God wants us to be. But this way of reading the Scriptures, if real change is to happen, has to become a part of your day-to-day lif

Your life won't change—you won't experience the power of a transformed mind—unless you make it a regular practice to spend time allowing the Bible to speak into the routines of your daily life. Then you will experience the power of God's Word hidden in the center of your being.

Notes

Chapter 1: The Choice between Two Paths

1. Louis Cozollino, *The Neuroscience of Psychotherapy* (New York: W. W. Norton, 2010), 312.

2. Bruce Lipton, *The Biology of Belief* (Carlsbad, CA: Hay House Inc., 2008), 129.

3. Ibid.

4. John L. Ratey, *A User's Guide to the Brain* (New York: Vintage Books, 2002), 209–14.

5. An example is Lee Huyssin and Jacquelynne Eccles, "Teacher Expectations II: Construction and Reflection of Student Achievement," *Journal of Personality and Social Psychology* 63, no. 6 (1992): 947–61.

6. Ellen J. Langer, *Counterclockwise: Mindful Health and the Power of Possibility* (New York: Random House, 2009), 120–22.

7. Lipton, *Biology of Belief*, 112.

8. Ibid., 109.

Chapter 2: The Physiology of Change

1. Norman Dodge, *The Brain That Changes Itself* (New York: Penguin Books, 2007), 10–12.

2. Buddy Levy, "The Blind Climber Who 'Sees' with His Tongue," *Discover*, July 2008, http://discovermagazine.com/2008/jul/23-the-blind-climber-who-sees-through-his-tongue.

3. Elkhonon Goldberg, *The New Executive Brain* (New York: Oxford University Press, 2009), 29.

4. Lipton, *Biology of Belief*, 121.

5. Candace B. Pert, *Molecules of Emotion* (New York: Scribner, 1997), 268–74.

Chapter 3: The ABCs of a Renewed Mind

1. Langer, *Counterclockwise*, 5–9.

2. Ibid., 11.

3. Charles Duhigg, *The Power of Habit* (New York: Random House, 2012).

Chapter 4: God's Plan for Our Transformation

1. Eugene Peterson, *Eat This Book* (Grand Rapids: Eerdmans, 2006), 18–19.

2. Ibid., 6.

3. James Finley, *Christian Meditation* (New York: Harper Collins, 2004), 72.

Chapter 5: Moving from Fear to Love

1. Psalm 27:1–3.

2. Psalm 91:4–6.

3. Psalm 112:7.

4. Isaiah 35:4.

5. Isaiah 41:10.

6. Isaiah 54:4.

7. Jeremiah 10:7.

8. Lamentations 3:57.

9. Ezekiel 2:6.

10. Romans 8:15.

11. Romans 8:38.

12. 2 Timothy 1:7.

13. 1 John 4:18.

14. Robert J. Sternberg, *The Triangle of Love* (New York: Basic Books, 1987).

15. C. S. Lewis, *Mere Christianity* (New York: Macmillan, 1952), 115.

16. John 13:35.

17. John 15:9.

18. John 15:13–14.

19. Romans 12:10.

20. Romans 13:8.

21. Romans 13:10.

22. Galatians 5:13.

23. Ephesians 4:31–32.

24. 1 Thessalonians 3:12.

25. 1 Thessalonians 4:9.

26. Hebrews 10:24.

27. 1 John 2:7.

28. 1 John 3:23.

29. 1 John 4:7.

30. 2 John 1:6.

Chapter 6: Moving from Anger to Forgiveness

1. Martin Luther, *Off the Record with Martin Luther: An Original Translation of the Table Talks*, trans. and ed. Charles Daudet (Kalamazoo, MI: Hansa-Hewlett, 2009), 110.

2. Exodus 34:6.

3. Psalm 30:5.

4. Psalm 103:8–9.

5. Ecclesiastes 7:9.

6. Proverbs 15:1.

7. Proverbs 19:11.

8. Proverbs 29:22.

9. Romans 12:17–19.

10. James 1:19–21.

11. Psalm 37:8.

12. Ephesians 4:26–27.

13. Redford Williams and Virginia Williams, *Anger Kills* (New York: Harper Paperbacks, 1993).

14. Numbers 14:18.

15. Matthew 6:12, 14.

16. Matthew 18:21–22.

17. Colossians 2:13–14.

18. Mark 11:25.

19. Ephesians 4:31–32.

20. Matthew 5:9.

21. Romans 5:1.

22. Romans 15:13.

23. 1 Corinthians 14:33.

24. 2 Corinthians 13:11.

25. Philippians 4:6–9.

26. Colossians 3:15.

Chapter 7: Moving from Loneliness to Connection

1. John T. Cacioppo and William Patrick, *Loneliness* (New York: W. W. Norton, 2008), 5.

2. Ibid., 15–16.

3. Ibid., 83–84.

4. Romans 13:8, 10.

5. Galatians 5:13–14.

6. Philippians 2:1–4.

7. Hebrews 10:24–25.

8. 1 Peter 4:8–9.

9. 1 John 3:23.

Chapter 8: Moving from Lust to Intimacy

1. "Pornography Statistics," Family Safe Media, 2013, www.familysafe media.com/pornography_statistics.html.

2. "Pornography," Women's Services & Resources, accessed August 26, 2013, wsr.byu.edu/pornographystats.

3. "Porn Sites Get More Visitors Each Month than Netflix, Amazon, and Twitter Combined," *Huffington Post*, May 4, 2013, http://www.huffington post.com/2013/05/03/internet-porn-stats_n_3187682.html.

4. United Families International, "14 Shocking Pornography Statistics," *The United Families International Blog*, June 2, 2010, http://unitedfamilies international.wordpress.com/2010/06/02/14-shocking-pornography -statistics.

5. "Pornography," Women's Services & Resources.

6. William Struthers, *Wired for Intimacy* (Downers Grove, IL: Inter-Varsity, 2009), 21.

7. Wendy Maltz, "Out of the Shadows," *Psychotherapy Networker*, November/December 2009, 56.

8. Naomi Wolf, "The Porn Myth," *New York*, October 20, 2003, 20.

9. 1 Corinthians 6:13.

10. 1 Corinthians 6:18.

11. 1 Corinthians 7:2.

12. 2 Corinthians 12:21.

13. Mark 7:20–23.

14. Galatians 5:19–21.

15. Colossians 3:5–6.

16. 2 Timothy 2:22.

17. 1 John 1:8–2:2.

18. Psalm 19:12–14.

19. Psalm 51:1–2, 7–10.

20. 2 Corinthians 7:1.

21. Titus 2:11–14.

22. Psalm 86:11.

23. Isaiah 52:11.

24. James 4:7–8.

25. Leviticus 22:32.

26. Romans 15:15–16.

27. 1 Thessalonians 4:7.

28. 1 Peter 1:16.

Chapter 9: Moving from Modern Idolatry to Contentment

1. Goodreads, "Quotes about Idolatry," http://www.goodreads.com /quotes/tag/idolatry.

2. James 4:3–5.

3. Colossians 3:5–6.

4. Ezekiel 6:9–10.

5. 1 Samuel 15:23.

6. Jonah 2:8.

7. 2 Corinthians 6:16.

8. Deuteronomy 29:18.

9. Proverbs 23:4–5.

10. Ecclesiastes 5:10–11.

11. Matthew 6:8.

12. Matthew 6:31–34.

13. Luke 14:33.

14. 1 Corinthians 10:14.

15. Philippians 3:19–20.

16. Philippians 4:6–7.

17. 1 Timothy 6:6.

18. 1 Timothy 6:8–11.

19. Hebrews 13:5.

20. 1 Peter 5:7.

21. 1 John 5:21.

Chapter 10: Moving from Life's Trials to Joy

1. Exodus 20:20.

2. Deuteronomy 8:2–3.

3. Psalm 66:8–12.
4. 2 Corinthians 4:16–18.
5. Colossians 1:24.
6. 2 Timothy 3:12.
7. Hebrews 10:35–36.
8. James 1:2–4.
9. 1 Peter 1:6–7.
10. 1 Peter 2:19–21.
11. 1 Peter 4:1–2.

Dr. David Stoop is the founder and director of the Center for Family Therapy. He is the author of more than twenty-five books, including *Forgiving the Unforgivable*. David and his wife, Jan, have coauthored books and lead worldwide seminars and retreats on topics such as marital relationships, parenting, men's issues, fathering, and forgiveness. They have three sons and six grandchildren. Learn more at www.Dr Stoop.com.

Find More Resources
and Connect with

DR. STOOP
@ DrStoop.com

MAKE A
POSITIVE CHANGE

What would happen if you applied the game-changing principles of emotional intelligence to your **most important relationship**?

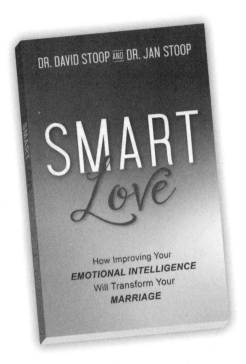

SMART Love is a system for understanding both your own and your spouse's emotions, managing those emotions, and walking hand in hand through situations when emotions run high.

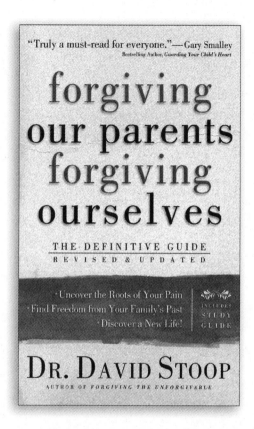

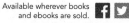

What do we do when confronted
with the unforgivable?

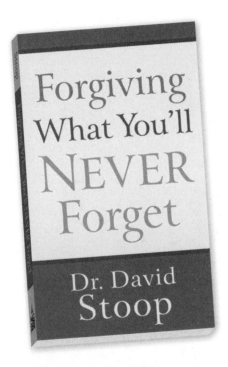

With deep compassion, clinical psychologist Dr. David Stoop shows
readers how to reap the emotional and spiritual benefits of forgiveness,
even when dealing with acts that seem unforgivable.